#RelationshipStatus

Thank You!

Nicah Mc~

# #RelationshipStatus

Nikki Akinyi McKenzie

NEW DEGREE PRESS

COPYRIGHT © 2021 NIKKI AKINYI MCKENZIE

#RelationshipStatus

ISBN    978-1-63676-839-7  *Paperback*

          978-1-63730-203-3  *Kindle Ebook*

          978-1-63730-283-5  *Ebook*

*To my family,*

*Thank you, for not questioning what the book is
about and encouraging me all along the way. I hope
that you enjoy it now that it is complete.*

*To my girls,*

*I am going to need a brunch date ASAP!*

*To Alexa,*

*Book tour is loading!*

*To Rodin,*

*Thank you for being there even when I didn't know I needed you.*

*Last but certainly not least,*

*To Mommy,*

*Thank you for being my role model and
teaching me to be unapologetically me.*

*To Daddy,*

*Thank you for the motivation and for being
in my corner every step of the way.*

# CONTENTS

———

*"Be careful, sometimes that sweet candy can be spiked with unexpected venom."*

"What do I want?"
I want something real
Something honest
Something open
Something forgiving
Something hopeful
Something full of promise, ambition,
and room for growth
Something that can hurt but also heal
We are human
Things will never be perfect
I don't want perfect, I want progression."

NICOLE A. MCKENZIE

# PART I

# WELCOME TO DATING

PART I

WELCOME TO
DATING

# THE SETUP

---

Let me set the scene for you.

**Time**: Pre-COVID

**Date**: November 25, 2018

**Place**: The couch, enjoying Sunday night football

**Mental Space**: Reminiscing on the bomb leftovers you had from Thanksgiving, a little sad they are gone, but you are a little thankful because who could take more turkey?

What am I doing, you may ask, besides staring at Odell Beckham Jr. run across the screen? I am trying to talk myself off the ledge from a potential battle. The phone is right there, and I keep glancing at it, shifting to the television.

**Two minutes**

Tap phone—it lights to a blank screen; my eyes shift back to a punt return on the screen.

**Five minutes**

The phone is in my hand, and I think to myself, maybe I missed a notification, knowing damn well I did not. The messages are still empty, and my last text has that "read" icon, mocking me.

Things descend quickly from there. The battle has begun. My brain goes a little something like this,

*I swear if he doesn't text me, he and I are going to fight.*
I pause and wait.

*He better not come to me tomorrow talking about,*
*"I'm sorry."*

*"You sir, I'm going to show you sorry. . ."*

Have you ever been in this predicament?

Sitting, waiting, and scheming your response to a conversation that's not going to happen, but just in case, you're ready.

Yeah, same. Terrible, I know.

Dating sucks, doesn't it? Even fake dating, the case of you being with someone without actually being with them.

Right now, dating has three perspectives:

1. It IS Trash
2. It IS Amazing
3. This IS Reality

It's trash to anyone that's single. Like, have you been on any dating apps? It's the Wild West out there! Side thought: have you ever realized the people who tell you to be patient about dating are all in relationships? Honestly, no sane single person would ever say that to another single person. To add insult to injury, following #relationshipgoals on social media leaves you daydreaming, but "this is reality." You question: *Why can't that be me? Look how happy and perfect they are.*

The reality is, dating is a terrifying combination of amazing and trash, it just depends where on the spectrum your relationship falls. There are so many aspects out of your control that it just comes down to the luck of the draw. If you are like me, you are probably still trying the apps or trying to navigate the dating world organically (which, if you have met someone not via your phone, can you please call me because I need advice). May the swipes ever be in your favor, or may the man buying you a drink actually call you back.

But what if he doesn't call? What happens when your texts are left on read?

I turned twenty-eight this year. I have been living a double life. I am Ms. Independent. I can take care of myself. I don't need someone to lean on. I get up and go without answering to anyone. But then, I lie awake at night scrolling and think, *Damn you are really alone, aren't you?*

I have considered settling, eating, not eating, moving into the gym, and thought: *What am I doing wrong?* I've talked to a guy, not talked to him. Forgiven one, and not forgiven the other. I feel as though I have tried it all and yet, here I am. I still have more questions than answers, and my cocktail of mixed emotions is enough to drive anyone crazy.

Through this chaos, I learned what I won't deal with, and the things I crave. Although I write this with no ring and no prospects, I can truly say that I am at least content with sharing my story and endless journey.

Truthfully, I think we are lying to ourselves, and some of us are . . . well, being a little selfish. It's not all men; some women straddle the line of being guilty of selfishness as well. Self-awareness is vital, and I think we all just need to be upfront with one another.

1. Why are we ghosting people?
2. Why are we acting as though our time is more valuable than anyone else's?
3. Why do we think our actions have no consequences?
4. Why are we acting as though emotions don't matter?

It has been scientifically proven, and it's in the word of God, that we as humans are not meant to be alone. From psychologist Guy Winch: "Loneliness is as bad for your health and longevity as smoking. It increases cholesterol, raises your blood pressure, and weakens your immune system. Spend too much time alone and you could literally be shortening your life."[1] In Genesis 2:18, the Lord God said, "It is not good that the man should be alone; I will make him an help for him."[2]

Why can't we just take care of each other and love each other the way we are meant to and how we all deserve?

We all have stories about trying to bridge the gap of finding our person. Some of us have had better experiences than others. For example, I am a young Black woman who has never fried chicken, and that apparently, to some, means I am never going to get a man. Statements like these and many other out-of-pocket things are my reality.

I want to speak on my experience with those who identify with me. Even if you don't see yourself, come along for the ride. For those in my shoes, I want to let you know that you aren't alone. I want women to feel included and men to realize some truths and relate to some tidbits as well. Writing, for me, is as therapeutic as mimosas. So, let's have a drink and share.

I pour this drink for you. (I also have tequila if you're interested.)

From the girl sitting at home curled up eating her Ben & Jerry's watching a basketball game, to the girl watching her rom-com, and the girl on FaceTime with her best friend wondering: *Is it just me?* This book is for those who feel like they don't want to be a burden but still want to be heard. Let me be your sounding board. Let this book guide you for any men wanting to know how some of their actions are being translated. For any men who have found themselves in this

---

1    Guy Winch, "Loneliness Poses Greater Public Health Threat than Obesity," *The Squeaky Wheel* (blog), *Psychology Today,* August 23, 2017.
2    Gen. 2:18 King James Version (KJV).

position, welcome. For any who may have answers to my endless questions, please, pull up a seat. Welcome to the Brunch Club—today's special is avocado toast with a side of real tea.

# HELLO

—

*Oh boy, please let me make it into this chair as gracefully as possible.*

"Hello."

*I hope that wave looked inviting and not as awkward as it felt.*

Ok, awkward hellos are out of the way, what's next on my list of awkward first date steps? I could ask them how they are doing, but that seems so basic, and ummm clearly, I can't ask them what's up. They are sitting right in front of me, so I know what is going on. Come on Nicole, you can't just sit here staring, you'll make a bigger fool out of yourself than you already are. *Sigh.* How about we go with honesty.

"Sorry, I haven't done this in a while."

*Oh dear God, please don't let my voice get any higher, soon only the dog outside will be able to hear me.*

See, that wasn't so hard. Now introduce yourself, you got this!

"My name is Nicole, thank you for being my date this evening. I hope this place is ok. I wanted to pick somewhere nice and quiet where we could get to know each other."

"How about we flip a coin to see who starts first? I call heads."

*Please be tails, please, please, please. . . Damn it!*

I guess I will start. My full name is Nicole Akinyi McKenzie. I am Afro-Caribbean, my mom is Kenyan, and my dad is Guyanese. I too was born in Guyana. I am thoroughly in love with my melanin, I strongly believe that thick thighs save lives, and Black girl magic is a very real thing. I mean, what else would explain the fact that our hair defies the laws of gravity?

*Look at you girl, sharp and witty. . . Keep going.*

At twenty-eight, I currently find myself single with no roster, no starting five, not even a third-round draft prospect. Just very, very single, and that's ok! I love my friends and family deeply and fiercely. You can catch these hands quickly over the people I love—I fight now and ask questions later. I am a stereotypical Pisces, which means I love love. It's practically cringeworthy. I continue to have faith in love, as disastrous as my love life has been. I still have hope—I know, shockingly—and you will too. Stick with me. I promise that no matter what happens, I will always keep it 100 with you.

I have put my love for people above my love for myself for years; I would rather do for others than do for myself. I find myself thinking, "What can I do to make them smile?" I pour into others without measuring how much they pour into me and without regard for what is left in my tank. My friends tell me to protect my space, my energy. But I don't think like that.

I am a hopeless, Pisces romantic. I don't think about what could go left because I am too hopeful about what could go amazingly right. I am too optimistic about capturing the love stories in oh so many R&B songs. As I sit here talking to you with my R&B Love Songs Pandora station bumping in the background, I can see flickers of two people embarking on a journey together and having the time of their lives, understanding and discovering their love journey. For me, if it's not love Babyface would write about, I do not want it.

Right now, all this love and hope is just all in my head. I am convinced I live in a world all my own. Through my experiences, people have convinced me that what I want is either too much or what I am aiming for is too high. They have brought on more questions than answers. However, the truth is that at the end of the day, I am just looking for someone to share this world with.

*Here goes nothing.*

So what about you? Would you be interested in taking this ride with me?

# WHO YOU GOT?

---

When I started dating a lovely young man named Derrick, who you will be getting a proper introduction to later on, one of my friends jokingly asked me once if he was my "first-round draft pick." As a sports lover, I always find it hilarious when people address dating as though they are building a roster. I guess that is what makes cuffing season so intriguing every year. I have not had the pleasure of actually "building a roster"; I tend to just have one star player at a time. You could say I like to focus my energy on one person, but truthfully, I have just never had the opportunity to be part of that life.

However, knowing myself now, it probably wouldn't have been the best of ideas anyway. I would like to take this time to introduce you to the men who have been team captains of a solo team throughout my dating life, or timeline, or journey, or whatever you want to call it.

There are a few men who will have a cameo, but they never stayed around long enough. I mean who cares about stats on a person that was only around for a one-week contract and still managed to stress you out? No thank you, we will not be revisiting those contracts again.

**Jonathan:** I've known him my whole life. Due to this and other connections, our relationship has been complicated. We tried to date, but it just wasn't a good time for us. He is in a relationship now, so great for him, but y'all, he was a piece of work.

**Kenny:** He was my first and so far, only success when it comes to dating apps. I was twenty-one at the time, and he was twenty-three going on twenty-four. We dated for about six months. After that, we had a pretty good friendship and still keep in touch from time to time.

**Derrick:** My tall glass of water, I am not afraid to admit that. I was twenty-three and he was twenty-six. He and I met at my job, and boy did he capture my heart with that smile of his. He made deliveries to our store weekly, and after months of staring, I finally manned up and said something, but we will get into that later.

**Pedro:** My best friend who I met in the ninth grade and who I have loved in varying degrees since. Saying it's complicated would be an overstatement because he is probably the easiest relationship I have ever had. He is my rock and a great support system. (Side note: he does have a girlfriend, so that's that.)

**Damien:** The love I found hiding under a friendship. We met randomly one night when I went to dinner with a friend, and we ended up developing a friendship from there. However, things changed when our friendship turned into something more, a "situationship" of a little over two years. Still trying to work through this one.

Please feel free to refer back at any time if you need a refresher, since even I sometimes get lost in my own stories and have to remember exactly which one of them I am referring to. This should be easier considering they are spread apart by actual years, but alas, one gets caught up in the emotion. Like the great Maya Angelou said, *"I've learned that people will forget what you said, people will forget what you did, but people will never forget how you made them feel."* [3]

---

3   Maya Angelou (@DrMayaAngelou), "I've Learned That People Will Forget What You Said, People Will Forget What You Did, but People Will Never Forget How You Made Them Feel," Twitter, September 2, 2018, 2:59 p.m.

# STANDARDS

---

*Hey Siri, define "standards."*

*According to Merriam-Webster, standards are "something established by authority as a rule for the measure of quantity, weight, extent, value, or quality."*[4]

Did you know there are ten different definitions of "standards," yet some of us, myself included, can't even stick to one? With all these definitions, I think I can boil standards down to one main synonym—expectations. Standards are the things or qualities that we expect out of someone.

Standards exist all around us, at work, at home, at the grocery store. For example, you expect your grocery store to carry Cheetos, and you know if they don't have any, you would be mad. Much like when I went to Giant last night and they were out of Cinnamon Toast Crunch—ruined my whole evening!

At work, you have your daily tasks and responsibilities, and you also check in with your boss from time to time—the guidelines are simple. That is what the beauty or pain (for some) of annual reviews are for. Personal standards include

---

4    *Merriam-Webster,* s.v. "standard (n.)," accessed February 10, 2021.

thoughts like "how presentable do I look today," "do I brush my hair," or "what clothes do I put on."

Since our focus is relationships, what are "relationship standards?" Is there a cue card for what standards make up a good relationship? Are the standards the same from person to person? Do the standards change from situation to situation? Considering the process of talking, to dating, to boyfriend and girlfriend, do the standards change as your relationship progresses?

Are there baseline standards? As you grow, different expectations are added on. Or are you one of those people who doesn't give two fucks and likes to go with the flow? (I am not saying this is a bad thing, I just know it's not for me. I learned that the hard way. Stay tuned for that lesson!)

I think standards are twofold—there are your basic-level foundational standards, which are the minimum requirements in any relationship. My basics include kindness, respect, communication, and honesty. Then, you have variable standards, which depend on the relationship or stage of the relationship you are in.

That's why mom always said, *Do not give your boyfriend husband privileges, because you should not hold your boyfriend to your husband's standards.* (If you are though, by all means, ignore me and carry on). For the rest of us, when we like someone, standards can get a little grey because we start thinking about the "what if," instead of the reality.

Let's take a step off the ledge, shall we, and dive into romantic relationships. They come in all forms, numbers, timelines, stages, and situations, but regardless of where you fall, I think there should always be some guidelines or common understanding, if you will. So, what is the bare minimum? In her article "Why Setting Standards in a Relationship is Mandatory," Leah Lee gives us amazing starting points.

"1. Expect the same respect you are giving.

2. Expect not to be treated as an option. *We know there are a lot of fish in the sea, you know what else is in the sea, trash. You, my lovely lady, should not come second to trash.*

3. Expect attention, affection, and time.

4. Expect an honest conversation.

5. Expect to be accepted for who you are."[5]

I believe that these standards are some simple things that anyone should expect out of a relationship, or any situation for that matter, but why does it seem that even expecting the bare minimum is "asking for too much"?

Thinking back, have you ever had a conversation with one of your girlfriends and either said or heard one of them say, "Yeah he actually texted me back, and we have been talking regularly"? Have you ever peeped the astonishment in their voice? Or when they go on a date and a guy pays and opens doors for them, like a Southern gentleman we thought only existed in movies?

For movie reference's sake, if you have seen *Think Like a Man,* Taraji P. Henson was being wined and dined by Michael Ely, even though he didn't have a lot of money. He just treated her like a queen in the best ways he knew how. (The way we should all be treated, might I add). Taraji was shook because Morris Chestnut, with all his money and good looks, wasn't giving her half that attention, and she did not know how to

---

5   Leah Lee, "Why Setting Standards in a Relationship Is Something Mandatory," *herway,* July 6, 2020.

act or feel with regard to the situation.[6] Acts of respect and kindness these days confuse us when, in reality, they are just the foundation.

When Derrick and I were together, he would text me, "Good Morning," at 5 a.m. just to check in because,

1. It was the only spare time he had.
2. He knew how important it was to me just to hear from him.

That simple two-word text was something I went on about for days to my co-workers. Thinking back now, when you can't even get a text back, gestures like that have a bigger significance.

I question though. . . Are we not taught that when we care about someone or like someone, we should show them? Actions speak louder than words, and we seem to be living in a world where people say a lot of things they don't mean.

Communication, kindness, respect, and honesty are my starter pack to any relationship/relationship-like situation.

Here is my big picture: if I am involved with someone, and we have mutually decided that we are going to try this whole dating/relationship thing, I should not have to beg to talk to him. The biggest argument I get about this is that people are busy. Trust me, I understand that everyone gets busy. I work three jobs and spend an hour in the gym almost every day, so I do get it. However, if you decide to hold a position in someone's life, in this case, mine, and if I find time for you, I expect the same courtesy. I am not expecting hour-long conversations every day. A simple "hello" or "hey, just checking on you" can go a very long way.

---

6    *Think Like a Man*, DVD, directed by Tim Story (2012, New York: Screen Gems, 2012)

Furthermore, I should not have to ask him to treat me like a person. I shouldn't have to ask for attention. Please keep this in mind for any men who may feel some type of way. This is high level. I understand there are different situations; some people can be clingy beyond normal expectations or needy, which goes way beyond basic attention. Right now, we are talking foundation. How am I supposed to get to know you if we don't spend any time together?

If individuals are not going to live up to their end of the bargain, theoretically we should let them go. That is why we have standards, right? However, most things in theory never quite play out the same in practice. Plus, life and people are never that easy. I have often found myself compromising, which is not to say that compromise as a whole is a bad thing. Relationships survive on compromise, but some things such as, I don't know, respect, shouldn't be negotiable.

When I have found myself compromising on the minimum, I questioned why. Was it a fear of being alone? Was it fear of losing that person? Was it wanting to keep my dinners? (I am kidding, I can pay for my own food.) I'm sure the answer will change depending on who you ask.

In my last situationship, I ended up compromising on communication. I adored Damien, but his lack of communication drove me crazy. He swore every time we had this issue, it would get better. Spoiler alert: it didn't. When you have had the same conversation with someone five times for two years, you kind of lose faith. Thinking back now, I feel dumb for even having the conversation more than twice.

Why compromise, you may ask? I compromised because I didn't want to lose him. I figured if I could just shut up and deal with it, everything would be ok. The messed-up part is, I lost him anyway. We find ourselves compromising on the foundation and then wonder where the cracks come from down the road. The cracks come from us when we start breaking our own bridge before it is built.

Compromise isn't inherently a bad thing; it's just how we use it. Take my situation, for example. My compromise came from wanting to keep this person in my life. In most instances, compromise comes from a supposed place of love. We fall into it for different reasons—wanting to end an argument, a need we have to be wanted, to be loved, or to have someone special give us attention. When we find someone with the potential to give us what we want, sometimes we take off with it a little prematurely. That is where the problems usually start; you ran with their potential, not the person who was standing in front of you. Don't get me wrong, some people will morph into that person you envisioned, but we cannot be shocked if they don't. We cannot force a change onto someone. They have to want to change for themselves. Like Leah said, "Expect to be accepted for who you are." We owe that guy or girl the same courtesy. If they switch up on you, then all bets are off.

Story time! In college, I had this light switch situation (on and off) with a guy named Jonathan. Jonathan and I were never officially anything, but we attempted to create a relationship for close to six months, at least that's how I describe the attempt. It is the kindest way to truly summarize the shit show that was those six months of my life. Jonathan is the person who first taught me how dangerous compromise is and exactly how things can boil over into a toxic situation.

When I look back, I always ask myself, "Nikki, how in the hell did you allow yourself to go through this?" The answer goes like this: In the beginning, I thought I saw something, and I thought he would change for me. I played myself! All that happened when this was over was that I never wanted to talk to him again. I was tired of him manipulating my emotions for his personal gain. Moving was the best thing that happened to me because it physically moved me out of his presence and him out of my life.

Quick six-month summary for better clarity: He and I were trying to get to know each other while living in the same area because for most of the on-and-off-again situationship, we lived in different states. During one of our offs, I started dating Kenny. One weekend, I was in town and ran into Jonathan. We ended up talking, and somehow, I ended up telling him about Kenny. . . He did not take it well.

We were having dinner, just enjoying a non-dramatic evening together. I am happily going to town on my mozzarella sticks as the Rockets and the Clippers game played in the background. My phone was on the table to my right. I was just about to ask him a question when my alarm went off.

"Why do you have an alarm set for 10 p.m.?"

Now here is where I had the opportunity to be an adult and could have easily explained it away as medication. However, my alternate ego Nikki came out to play, and she decided to be a smartass.

"It's none of your business, but if you must know, it was for my birth control."

"Why would you need that, 'cause it's not like you wanted to give it up to me."

"Not to you but someone else."

I looked him dead in the eye and finished the Coke that was in my hand with a slight tilt in my head. Was I a bitch? Absolutely. Do I regret it? At the time, no, and even now not really. We had been gearing up for a fight for so long, it was inevitable. Don't get the wrong idea, he was not pushy about the sex issue but always questioned why I wouldn't sleep with him. The answer was easy: I wanted the commitment that he wouldn't give. I didn't get what I wanted, and you certainly weren't going to either.

He never let that go, as though he wasn't out here sleeping with who-knows-who when I wasn't around. But back to the story, I left for school, came back after graduation, and against my better judgment, decided to give it a chance. We were fine in the beginning, but then he would pick little fights or start talking to all these different girls, and I just couldn't do it. And whenever I brought up a girl, he would try to throw Kenny back in my face, and you see that right there? Nope! It took me about two fights to see the manipulation, because at first, I tried to be empathetic about it. After the third time, it made me so angry to the point I went to a parking lot and screamed. That was my blinker signaling the start of a change. The actual turn happened thanks to my best friend Logan. After I finished ranting to her about his most recent shenanigans, she told me, "Don't let his insecurities ruin something that you hold deep in your heart."

If you can't respect my past for what it is—the past—the way I respect yours, then what are we even doing? Fortunately for me, there was one girl in particular who he latched onto out of his plethora of women. I decided to let her keep him. I was not going to be anyone's plan B. Lucky for me, a few weeks later, I got a job, and I was out.

Future take for you guys: When I went home about two or three years ago, I saw Jonathan, and the conversation we had stuck with me forever. He was leaning on my car, arms crossed in front of his chest, and he just kept looking at me before he finally opened his mouth.

"Would you consider getting back together with me?"

"First, you have to actually be together with someone to get back with them, and second, do you not have a girlfriend?"

"That was going to change."

"You think so?"

"Yeah, I do."

*Eye roll.* Y'all, they are still together. Do you see why I may or may not have issues with men? Anyway, moving on . . .

Pre-Jonathan, I used to think I was high maintenance. Now, I just think we live in a time of some weird off-the-wall thinking.

At the time I am penning this chapter, I am twenty-seven years old, on the way to twenty-eight. I have dated and talked to some folks but never quite got to "relationship status."

I had friends and dates before they became dates. Ask me why I don't or have never had a boyfriend? My response to this question has changed over the years. It started with, "I don't know," because honestly, I didn't and still don't. The response then morphed into: "He decided to date another girl," (this is a product of my 2016 dating phase, which we will get into later on), "I'm not interested in anyone," etc. My most recent response, when asked, was, "Because apparently consistency and communication are too much to ask for."

Depending on the day, if you ask me how I feel about my single status, you will either get a joyful smile that translates into, "I am happy, just working on myself and growing," a shoulder shrug that means "I am ok with where I am at, but a good date would be nice too," or a grimace, which means "Why am I alone?" *Please bring me a tub of half-baked ice cream from Ben & Jerry's.*

I am at a point in my life where I have friends getting married and having kids, and I want that, too. People in my life want that for me as well. Family is always asking questions about your personal life. Yikes! Even though the feelings are dependent, on the situation and they grow, one thing that won't be growing anymore is basic standards. Either you step up to the plate wholeheartedly or you keep it pushing. As much as I do not want to be, I am a player in this game too.

That is why I have my standards. You can think of it as rigid or think I have an attitude for not following your way. It is my safety; it is how I keep myself from falling into something that isn't right for me. Relationships come with no guarantee, but I can at least try and start on a good foundation. Ladies, ask yourself what is that you want in a relationship and build from there because your standards are the foundation that the relationship stands on. Gentleman, you should do the same.

Establish them and stick to it (well, at least try to, I know it's one of those things that, depending on that smile he is throwing at you, can be easier said than done). It is ok, if you slip, we will be here to catch you and remind you why you should never do that again!

"Strong women don't have 'attitudes,' we have standards."[7]

**THE LIST HAS TO GO, SIS!**

Plot twist: we are not done. Ladies, I am so sorry to do this to you, but some of us need to be stopped. Why, may you ask? That is because some of us have taken the word standards and ran three miles with it, confusing foundational necessities with superficial wants.

---

7    Emily Blackwood, "Strong Women Don't Have 'Attitudes' - We Have STANDARDS," *Mind Journal*, October 19, 2020.

Have you ever asked yourself, "What is it that you want in a man?" If not, I want you to ask yourself that question right now and write it down.

.

.

.

.

.

.

.

Ok, stop. Are you still listing the things that you want in a man? If so, does it sound like a two-week quarantine grocery list?

Please do not get me wrong. I am not saying that you do not deserve a man who treats you well, is able to provide, and who is kind and honest. However, some of us have gotten a little too nitty-gritty and specific, maybe ruining our blessing in the process. Your "requirements" in a man should never look like a CVS receipt. There is a difference between having standards, like the non-negotiable ones we addressed. Some include:

1. Respect
2. Communication
3. Honesty
4. Loyalty

The list may vary by person. These make sense.

However, some lists may look more like this:

1. Tall, 6'o average
2. Good job
3. Benefits
4. Drives an Audi 300, preferably in red
5. Likes Drake

6. Gets pedicures every two weeks
7. Likes mochas with a hint of caramel
8. Cooks

Sound familiar?

I do not mean to out you—I too used to be, and sometimes still am, one of those people. I am working on it though.

There is a huge difference between having non-negotiable standards, because every relationship needs a strong foundation, and having a list as though you are going to Target. One is protection and the other is just being picky. We are allowed to be picky, but much like everything in life, it has its limits. I am guilty of it too, so don't feel attacked, I am just here to help.

Back in May, I heard the greatest piece of advice on a Sunday afternoon from the pastor of Transformation Church, Pastor Michael Todd, and it was RIP THE LIST.[8] The list has to go, sis. You could be holding yourself back from your best blessing because he only checks five of your twenty-eight boxes.

Without getting too religious about things, the main takeaway is that there is a clear distinction between what we want and what we need. In this particular sermon, Pastor Mike talks about ripping up the list so that God has the opportunity to place in our life what we need—not what we "think" we need.

Even if looking at it this way is not your cup of tea, we can get secular about it as well. How many of us get on Instagram and look at images on TV and YouTube videos of couples and think to ourselves, "Yeah that is what I want?"

---

8    Transformation Church, "Rip Up Your List (Part 1)," May 3, 2020. video, 1:15:05.

The #relationshipgoals hashtag stays viral. We all now want that picture-perfect image that social media created, and now we feel to get that picture-perfect image, we need that picture-perfect man.

One of my favorite celebrity couples is Ayesha and Steph Curry. I can swipe through their IG pages for days and ooh and ahh at how adorable they are together. Here is the part most of us don't think about unless we are going to be with that person: we are not going to have the same relationship! We have to ground our expectations in reality; the keyword here is to *build*, not settle.

This relationship "guru" that I follow on Facebook and IG called Derrick Jaxn (I know but I wrote this pre-scandal) did a talk on male expectations of women (we will get into this when we talk about societal pressures) and said, "Men say they want an Ayesha Curry, but are you Steph? Meaning that how can you expect a woman to give herself to you like Ayesha does if you aren't providing her with Steph Curry-like benefits."[9]

I hate to be the one to call any woman out, but let's flip this around. If a man is giving you Steph energy, doesn't that mean you also need to step up to the plate? The truth is women can also have unhealthy expectations of men. You end up falling for an idea and not the person in front of you. Then, you are mad at him for not giving you YSL shoes for your birthday knowing very well he does not have YSL money! (That was a dramatic analogy, but you get my point.)

We need to normalize real relationships, not just the fancy, staged images that permeate through our phones. As much as

---

9   Derrick Jaxn, "My Thoughts on Guys Who Say 'I Need Me an Ayesha Curry,'" *Derrick Jaxn* (blog), June 16, 2017.

we want, we cannot all marry NBA or NFL players. However, that does not mean you cannot find yourself a good man who completes you.

When developing this chapter, my developmental editor made a great point. I doubt I fit into anyone's "checklist" completely. So, who am I to expect all these exaggerated expectations from someone else? I doubt someone's checklist reads:

- 5'4
- Average-ish but curvy
- Crazy
- Hair defies the laws of gravity
- Super shy, yet has a resting bitch face
- Slight fear of the dark
- Eats pineapple on pizza
- Addicted to the gym but thinks ice cream should be a food group

We need to be more open-minded about each other because the world operates in mysterious ways. For example, my best friend who got married a few months ago; when you see pictures of her and her husband, you would think they walked off a *GQ* cover together—it's making me tear up even thinking about it. However, when they met, he wasn't even on her radar. He wasn't who she was looking for. Fun fact: she disliked him when they first met and didn't want much to do with him.

However, after some persistence on his end and her becoming more open-minded, you now have this happy couple who own a gorgeous home in Louisiana. Do yourself a favor and rip up the list. It really could change your life. Sure, things may take some time, but once again, here's a friendly reminder from Pastor Mike: "Delayed doesn't mean denied."[10]

---

10   Michael Todd (@iammiketodd), "Delayed Doesn't Mean Denied," Twitter, May 12, 2020, 3:18 p.m.

# PART II

# WHAT IS DATING?

# WHAT DOES DATING
# EVEN MEAN?

———

*"Talking stage: Two years*
*Relationship: Five years*
*Engagement: Three years*
*Plan the wedding: One-and-a-half years*
*Get married"*[11]

I came across this tweet a few months ago, and according to this math, if by some grace of God, I meet someone who may actually be interested in the crazy that is 2020, I won't be married until I'm pushing thirty-eight! I just want to know who came up with this timeline, because I would like to reclaim my time even though it has not happened yet.

Regardless of how long anyone decides to stay in these stages, this generally sums up the phases of modern-day dating and relationship progression.

———

11   Penthousepapi (@primehob), "Talking Stage 2 Years relationship 5 Years Engagement 3 Years Plan the Wedding 1.5 Years Get Married," Twitter, June 13, 2020, 12:19 a.m.

Talking alone has many subsections. For example, we could be talking, but are we exclusively talking to each other, or are we talking and still entertaining other people? When the entertainment stops and exclusivity is reached, are we boyfriend and girlfriend? Or do we need to talk some more before labels are attached?

Labels themselves require a conversation. How important are labels to this particular situation? Are we labeling ourselves or are we labeling this "thing" that we have going on? I have heard the argument over labels go both ways. Some say that labels make things complicated, and others have felt that labels are important to understand where a person's mind is at and how their actions should be perceived.

Personally, I agree with the latter. I thrive on labels. Labels provide much-needed reassurance that helps me understand what I am involved in, and they can also help keep my insecurities from making an unwanted appearance. That is why I like labels, so I have my receipts and can just push them back to where they came from.

Nowadays, one can take so many avenues in dating; there are too many forks in the road to count. Dating itself has become so complicated. I would love to go back to a simpler time. When my parents started seeing each other, there was no talking stage. You were just dating, and this whole "exclusivity versus non-exclusivity," yeah, that didn't exist either. Dating = relationship. That was it!

I am not saying that this happened immediately. No, you can't force something that is not there. Getting to know someone and letting your relationship grow organically is important. However, they didn't have questions like, "What are we doing?" It was very clear what was going on!

When Derrick and I stopped talking, I tried to retroactively explain what had happened to my mom. She asked me if I was dating him. To which I responded:

*No.*

She then countered with,

*So what were you doing with him?*

Honestly, great question, mom. My mom and dad got together in a time where the process of dating was very clear. Y'all were either together or not together, case closed. As much as I am here for people figuring out what they want, I miss the simplicity of this time. All the if, buts, and maybes make it so that no one, not even the people involved, know what's happening or what to do.

I myself have been caught in these waves of uncertainty. When I talk to someone, I do it with the intention of seeing if it can lead somewhere, not to just aimlessly be blowing in the wind. I realize I have been that way even back in college.

When I was in high school, I didn't date, but not for lack of trying. High school boys were not into me, and this pattern pretty much repeated itself in college with the exception of one person.

In my mind, college was the place I was going to meet my future husband. I had built this whole scenario in my head—it's quite comical when I think about it now. The joys of being young and naïve.

Anyway, by the time senior year rolled around, my dreams had been dismantled, and I was ready to try anything to meet someone new, hence my progression to the apps that led to my meeting with Kenny.

If I remember correctly, I sent the first message, which is so very unlike me. I lose like fifteen brain cells when I talk to men, even virtually. He thought my rambling was cute, so for once, awkward worked out in my favor.

We chatted about our love of sports, I learned that he was a Maryland native, and we shared random tidbits about each other. The highlights of my day were seeing the little blue notification pop up on my phone whenever he had messaged me back.

After about a week, he asked me out on a date. We bounced a few ideas back and forth about our date location and eventually settled on dinner. I met him at a restaurant (you know, safety first) so we could have our date in a public place. We had dinner at a Red Lobster.

Sidebar: Want to know something funny? I now live up the street from that very same Red Lobster! Who would have thought?

I tried to find a good balance between "I am this cute every day" and "I put in effort for our date" vibes. I settled on a loose cream sweater, black leggings, and a pair of Vince Camuto boots. He met me outside the train station, looking casual but FINE in his fitted orange t-shirt, jeans, and leather jacket.

I spotted him before he saw me. Let me tell you, he was so much cuter in person. I could tell he was looking for me; he ended up walking past me because of where I was standing in the metro. I called after him

"Looking for someone?"

He pivoted and looked at me and just started to laugh. I like to think it was a great first impression. We all want humor in our relationships, right?

We started to walk and talk. About halfway to the restaurant, he slowly reached my hand, and I met him halfway. There were butterflies, obvious nervousness, but no awkwardness. At the restaurant, he ran through three glasses of water in ten minutes, the waitress was dumbfounded, and I laughed at her expression.

We talked about his practice (he ran track) and my studies and bonded over our love for cartoons. It was a memorable first date. He drove me back to campus, lightly drawing patterns on my knee the whole ride back. We spent the night in my room watching *Looney Tunes* and making out (damn, the man was a good kisser)—but pump your brakes, nothing happened. . . that night.

As the weeks went on, he met all of my close friends, and they all loved him. Friend test: check! They all thought that he was sweet and attentive, which he was. Plus, he was very cuddly, I just enjoyed moments sitting in his lap and talking about our days. He worked about ten minutes away from my school, and he would come spend the afternoon with me before he worked his night shift. He was off Wednesdays and would stay with me Wednesday nights into Thursday mornings. Whatever time he could make for me, he gave to me willingly, no questions asked.

I had one very awkward experience meeting his mother. She was very sweet—it's just that meeting her at midnight because she answered the door instead of him was not the way I wanted to start my evening, or morning, whichever way you want to look at it.

Kenny and I had a deal while his car was in the shop. I would drive out to get him and he would drive back to my place. We were planning our usual Friday evening of dinner and cartoons. I called him when I was leaving so he could get ready, and then I hit the road. When I got there, he wasn't answering his phone. I started to panic mostly because I wasn't about to drive here and then all the back to DC for nothing. I sat in the car and blew up his phone for fifteen minutes. After that, I just sat there faced with a dilemma. I could go home, or I could put on my big girl pants and go ring the damn doorbell. Brave Nikki won that night. I got out of the car slowly and walked to the door, praying he would call me back before I got there.

Alas, he did not, so I took a deep breath and rang the bell. Mind you, it was about 11 p.m. at night, so this was already looking bad. Add the fact it was below 50 degrees outside— the evening just kept getting better and better. (I am from Florida, so anything below 60 degrees is cold).

An older woman opened the door, peering out slightly perplexed as to who was ringing her doorbell at 11 p.m. She stared at me for a moment longer than deemed appropriate, which she had every right to do because who was I, and why was I at her door at 11 p.m.?

I stared back at her trying to stop myself from turning around and running away. I proceeded instead to take a breath and asked if Kenny was here. (Side note: I only did this because he knew I was coming). She said yes, turned into the home, and then gave me this over-the-shoulder-glance before hollering for him. Five seconds later, I heard the scrambling of feet up the stairs, and he appeared at the door. He at least had the decency to look contrite for putting me in this mess. He apologized profusely, I accepted, and we went on with our evening. The tale was that he had fallen asleep while waiting for me and didn't hear his phone. What a way to meet the parents, right? My hands start shaking even when I think about it now.

In my naïveté, I thought we were moving toward something, that he would soon ask me to be his girlfriend. I was giddy with the prospect of having my first boyfriend. As you can all guess, the giddy feeling ran out, coming to a grinding halt.

We had been talking for about two or three months when I decided to ask the dreaded question of, "What are we doing?" His response was, "I was reading into things a little too much," and that he didn't want a relationship. Wish I would have asked this question before I had slept with him. I chalk this whole situation up to the fact that you live and learn. I built something in my head that was not the reality in front of me and got my feelings hurt.

Our disbandment hurt me, and I was stuck in my head for a while, asking myself how I got into this position in the first place. The answer is, I wasn't clear on my expectations, which I can't blame myself for at the time because I really did not know any better. I just wanted to be what he wanted. At the time, what he was doing was enough until it wasn't. Did I make the same dumb ass mistake again? Absolutely, but that also had its own set of love lessons that I don't regret, either.

He and I stopped talking as often, and about two months later, he ended up moving to Texas. Interesting thing is we never totally cut off contact. I knew all about his girlfriend in Texas and their situation. That is their tea and not my business to share. However, they did eventually part ways. One summer, I was very, very bored and decided to take an impromptu trip to Austin. You know who else lives in Austin . . . Kenny. Let's just say weekend reconciliations can be such a fun time. He was a true Southern gentleman who showed me around the city and paid for all our meals. Really showed your girl a good time.

About two months later is when we start our journey with Derrick. We will get into a deep dive on Derrick later on, but with him in the beginning, he told me he was not ready for a relationship, and I accepted that. Then about two weeks later, he stopped talking to me because he was now in a relationship with someone else. So, the real tea was that you wanted a relationship, just not with me. Understood. I went home and cried, peacefully, while watching my favorite show and eating a pint of Tonight Dough from Ben & Jerry's. (Mine was *CSI* at the time—love crime dramas.)

When I talk about Kenny or Derrick, I always have to preface it with all these long, drawn-out explanations of how we talked or kind of dated but were never really together. After all that, now I can explain the story about them. This is supposed to be a conversation, not a thesis on who this man was in my life. Why do I need an introduction, three supporting paragraphs, and a conclusion to explain the fact that we were but also were not?

Another thing is not just explaining who they are but also what the parameters were of these relationships. Are we exclusive or not? If we have not established what "this" is, at what point do others stop being involved? And if others just fall off naturally but after a few months, one pops into your life and piques your interest again, what happens then? Are you allowed to entertain them? Is that wrong? I know I am asking a lot of questions, but I am honestly asking for a friend. At the end of the day, the core of dating labels or no labels, exclusivity or not all still boils down to communication and consistency. Is the energy still right, and are we addressing what on Earth is going on with us?

In understanding dating, my one piece of armor in this field is always asking what a person's intentions are. I learned this from Kenny. Labels or not, it will give me a good read on whether or not our end goals are aligned. If you are looking to still entertain two other women, plus me, then I am good.

We do not even need to "talk." I know what I am looking for, and many nights I swear I am not going to find it in my generation.

My parents met on a bus. My dad had to be talked into asking my mom out because he was not sure that she would be interested. He took the time and effort to plan a sweet first date for them. Do you realize that in the time before phones, texting, ghosting, and leaving people on read, if you dated someone who did not live in your area, you would have to write them letters? Actually, sit down with a pen and paper, find an envelope and stamps, go to the post office, and mail it. Relationships held strong, yet somehow, in this day and age with all this accessibility and ease of contact, I can't even get a five-letter *hello* text, or, if you are really in a time crunch, a three-letter *hey*. I just want to know when wanting to establish something real went out of style. When effort became such a hardship. I guess that comes with the dating game now, figuring out the pieces and fitting them together.

Dating has a different answer depending on who you ask. If you ask Google, the response is someone in whom one is romantically or sexually interested.[12] My favorite definition of dating has to come from *Urban Dictionary*, though: "Dating is where two people who are attracted to each other spend time together to see if they can stand to be around each other most of the time, if this is successful, they develop a relationship, although sometimes a relationship develops anyway if the people can't find anybody else to date them, or are very lonely or one person is only attracted to the other and

_____

12    *Oxford Languages*, s.v. "dating," Google Search. Google, accessed January 21, 2021.

pretends to be in love with the second unfortunate person who has the misunderstanding that they have found love."[13]

See, even the internet cannot fully agree on what dating is, so clearly, we as people are never going to figure that out. *Urban Dictionary* really exposed us to the tomfoolery of dating with that explanation.

Dating has its complexities, but I still think it's worth it. I will never fully understand it, but I can discern what I want out of it. Once we can establish what we want and what we are looking for, the next step is finding someone to match that energy. Dating is not a perfect science, and we all know that we will probably have to go through some storms or hardships, whatever you want to call it to get there.

Even if that takes some time, that's ok. Figuring out dating is not a race, regardless of what your family has to say about your current relationship status. You know how family always wants to be all in your business.

---

13   *Urban Dictionary*, s.v. "dating," accessed January 21, 2021.

# SO, DO YOU HAVE A BOYFRIEND?: FAMILY EDITION

---

I feel as though from this title alone, most of you can guess where I'm going with this. However, if you are one of the select few who has never been questioned by their family, please count your blessings. Not only is it awkward and embarrassing, but it is also emotionally draining.

I tend to get these questions from my extended family and my parent's friends, who are essentially family, too. The people who, if I see them once a year, it is still a lot. The people who should just be enjoying this brief time we have together instead of worrying about some new person who could "potentially" make our family larger.

Have you ever been to a family gathering, and all of sudden it gets quiet, and your aunt from across the way hits you with any or all of the following left-field questions?

- "Are you seeing anyone?"
- "What happened to [insert name here]?"

- "Why aren't you seeing someone?"
- "How long have you been single now?"

After she asks the question, there is this extended pause because your brain is trying to figure out how you got here. We were just talking about grandma; how did stories of grandma turn into what my relationship status is and is not? *Do I look unhappy? Why is this any of your business? If you were supposed to be in the know, you would know.* It makes me want to scream.

In my case, the answer is:
- No.
- We are not together.
- I don't know.
- It's been a few years.

All these responses cumulate into the deep burning question in your relative's mind, and maybe the one in your own mind: WHY IS YOU SINGLE? (I know it's supposed to say *are*, but I said what I said!)

Dear family and family adjacent, I do not really know what to tell you because quite frankly I can't really answer that question. I am still trying to figure out my singleness, to be honest. It is a very loaded question. Does anyone really ever know "why" they are single unless it is a conscious decision? How about we do this, if you feel as though you know the answer, please leave a card in the suggestion box, and we can suspend this unnecessary interaction for another six to twelve months.

I only speak from experience, and here it is. Back in 2016, I moved back to the DC-Maryland-Virginia area (DMV). I went to school in DC and having the opportunity to move back felt like returning to my second home. Added bonus, one of my mom's best friends, who is like an aunt to me, lived nearby. Throughout school, I would go over to her house for home-cooked meals and reality TV binge weekends, it was a great time.

We do have to take a quick step back, though. You guys remember Kenny? If you need a quick refresher, flip back to "Who you got?" (I'll wait.)

You know, Kenny and I had our moments together when I was at school. He ended up moving, and that was that, for now. One weekend, I went over to my aunt's house for food, good company, and trashy TV. It was supposed to be an escape. I was new in corporate America, just trying to get by, and men were the furthest thing from my mind. The only thing I wanted was to understand my leasing agreement.

Sidebar: For all the money we spend in school to aid in securing a career, why does it not teach you how to lease an apartment or understand your taxes? You know, real-world experiences that you actually need. Pythagoras is not paying my bills.

It was an amazing afternoon of *Keeping Up with Kardashians* and *The Real Housewives of Potomac*. Things were going so well, until that pause settled in and she swung that bat left field.

Somewhere deep in the midst of another *Real Housewives* episode scandal, my aunt turns to me and pauses. With that alone, I should have known this was coming. . .

"So, are you dating anyone?"

"No."

This should have been the end of the discussion, right? I mean, there is perfectly good fake/real drama on the screen, making our lives look like a cakewalk. However, nope! She then followed up with. . .

"What about Kenny?"

Wait, what! How do you still even remember who he is? I had not thought about him in months, why is he on your mind?

"He moved back home. Long distance wasn't an option."

For extension's sake, this should be it, case closed. A normal response would have been

"Ok, I was just wondering."

However, my family, like most, does not abide by normal. She continued on. . .

"Well why didn't you move? What are you still doing here?"

I am pretty sure I just stared at the center of her forehead for five seconds and then proceeded to laugh. Excuse me, what! I was supposed to pick up my very fragile life; at the time he left, I still had six months of school. However, let's say for argument's sake she is talking about now, post-graduation. My whole life was contained in three suitcases, and I was supposed to follow a man who wasn't even actually my boyfriend? We were still only talking or whatever the heck it is we were doing at the time. No, nope, that is not what I was going to do. By the way, fun fact, at the time he was dating another girl, so that was a whole moot point.

The people in my life love swinging left, just for their enjoyment at my awkward pain. Here's another more recent example of the questions. . .

One night I called my aunt (a different aunt from earlier; in Black families everyone is your auntie, but this conversation happened with my actual aunt). I was at work, and a difficult customer came in, and I just needed to vent about this interaction with someone, so I called her.

"OMG, I have to tell you what just happened to me!"

"What, what happened?"

"This woman just came into the store and started yelling."

"Oh, I thought you were calling to tell me you met the love of your life."

*Facepalm.* I mean how, who, what, when, where, why? I mean as nice as that would have been, why was that your first thought when I called you at 5:30 p.m. in the afternoon?

Isn't spending time with family supposed to be about togetherness and bonding? Yet somehow it tends to become a Spanish Inquisition on (well at least in my case) my love life. Like, why does everything in my life have to lead back to my lack of a significant other? I had just gotten my first post-college job; can we please celebrate that with a glass of wine instead of side-eyeing the rim as though I have done something wrong?

The other side to this is when the family tries to flip the script on you. When you have nothing to say about your life, they ask you questions about your friends. I came across this tweet that sums up this discussion perfectly.

"Real convo:

Mom: Are you dating anyone?

Me: No.

Mom: (Long ass pause) . . . Well, are your friends dating anyone?"[14]

I am sorry, were you actually concerned or are you just looking to gossip? Are you going to try and shade me about my lack of a love life by comparing me to friends? You know what, [insert relative here], you can go have a conversation with them. I would no longer like to be the middleman in your quest to find out the world's relationship status. What

14   Amanda Brooke Perrin (@brookeperrin), "Real Convo: MOM: Are You Dating Anyone? ME: No.MOM: (LONG ASS PAUSE) ... Well, Are Your Friends Dating Anyone?," Twitter, September 20, 2017, 7:18 p.m.

happened to you not being worried about my little friends like my mom?

Regardless of whether they are asking about you specifically or your friends, this conversation as a whole is emotionally draining. Besides, it really builds frustration in me and makes me feel as though I need to defend myself for something that is pretty out of my control. Admittedly, I am an overthinker by nature. I've gotten better, but it's a progression. What tends to start to happen is a downward spiral where I start to question myself,

"Why am I single?"

Maybe they have a point, and it has been too long, and something is wrong. Maybe something is wrong with me? I start to think about my "Wallflower Syndrome," meaning that compared to the people I know and am friends with, I tend to fall in the back and be unnoticed when they are around. It honestly gets worse from there. Is it because I'm not pretty enough, nice enough, in good enough shape? Why do I keep showing up alone? Now I find myself back in the rabbit hole, having to slowly dig myself out and remind myself that is ok. Deep breaths!

So, I have a PSA!

Dear family, here is the answer. No, I'm not seeing anyone. I'm just living my life right now. Sure, I want someone to come along, but I want them to be the right someone. In the meantime, Nikki (me) is going to take Nicole (also me) on an ice cream date!

Ice cream is my general coping mechanism, not the healthiest thing in the world, but that's why I go to boxing class. Honestly, though, the best advice I can give when it comes to these types of questions is to laugh it off.

We are not living in an era of arranged marriages anymore, so no one can dictate your timeline for relationships but you. If you are single right now, with no intentions of dating, amazing. If you are single and looking, great! If you have a little something going on that you are not quite ready to share, honey that is your business and no one else's.

The next time they ask, shrug your shoulder, throw them a kilowatt smile and say, "Don't worry about it, you will know when you need to know." Response option two comes via the lovely land of Twitter. "When people ask me, 'So, are you seeing anyone?' I am just going to say, 'Yes: A therapist.'"[15]

Of course, though, when the time comes that someone does walk into my life, I am sure the questions won't disappear—they will just transform into the following:

- "How long have you been dating?"
- "What is his family like?"
- "Are you guys going to get married?"

Same ole family, just a different status.

---

15  Julia Pugachevsky, "22 Jokes You'll Get If Your Family Constantly Asks About Your Love Life," *Cosmopolitan*, December 26, 2017.

# THIS GENERATION ISN'T FOR ME

---

As much as I enjoy being a '90s baby and living through this particular time period, sometimes I question if this is really where I belong.

*Are my views on dating old-fashioned?*

*Will I meet someone in person or is online dating my only option?*

*Why is dating more like a game of chess than an experience to enjoy?*

These questions vary from swipe to swipe, as I have been involved in the online realm of dating even though that is not what I want. I would love to meet someone just doing boring everyday shit like buying Baked Cheetos at the grocery store! Yes, I have watched entirely too many movies, but the point still stands; is that too much to ask for? Online dating is such trash, I dedicated a two-part chapter to it.

My generation has been robbed of dating experience and it shows. Dating apps have corrupted many of us, one way or another. I personally am guilty of it as well. Online dating has boiled us all down to a photograph and a few words when we as individuals are so much more complex. In this simplified realm, no one has a fair shot anymore. No one can really be themselves; some folks online truly are not themselves. Actions like this lead everyone to have their walls up, and the swipes just become a game. We are playing each other like a game of checkers looking to win, but honestly, at the end of the day, what is the prize?

- A few new notches on your bed?
- A collection of broken hearts?
- Earning the title of player?

I am on the apps. I do not like it, but I am present. Foundationally, I do not have a problem with the apps themselves. It is just a new way to facilitate relationships. For me, I just crave an organic experience. Right now, I am at a 50/50 split on whether or not I will get my wish. I will continue to pray about it, and I will keep you guys posted. There is something about meeting someone organically that I think we take for granted.

Meeting someone in person, you can sense a person's vibe, something you cannot discern through a computer screen. You can pick up on body language when they speak and actually hear and understand their tone and voice. With miscommunication happening all the time in text, I can only imagine what can happen in messages back and forth with a person you are trying to get to know. These are just a few examples. The point is, we have been robbed and don't even recognize it.

I want a story like my parents'. They are going to celebrate their thirty-year anniversary in 2021. They have made it through trials and tribulations. Good days and the bad while still finding a way to make it through together. To think a long-standing story like theirs, with many more years to come, all started with a simple glance on the bus is heart-warming. My parents (shout out to Esther and Brian McKenzie) were both studying at the University of Kiev. My dad received his master's in aeronautical engineering, and my mom received hers in international affairs. One day, my mom was out with her friends on their way to the market, and my dad was already on the bus when she and her friends boarded. He caught a glimpse of my mom from across the aisle and was immediately intrigued. There are details of this meeting they both still refuse to share, but that was the start of their journey. A connection like this that is fostered through a curious glance or a look of intrigue does not come through a screen. That pull and desire to learn more about the person that just crossed your path. That is pure human chemistry.

*Is it bad that I want that?*

A moment, a journey, with so many elements to it that obviously makes for great writing. This is what I grew up with, a love that took time and work. A spark of intrigue developed into a bond that withstood moving to different countries and spending years apart. A connection of substance and value. Right now, it is hard for me to see that happening through my phone when my inbox is usually full of messages such as:

"Ur a sexy, thick wife size baby"

Excuse my language, but what the fuck does that even mean?

One, can we please use proper sentence structure? Proper English is attractive.

Two, "thick wife size baby"? I just, I can't with the male population sometimes—I just can't!

This is a little off topic, but it still relates to the messages. One of my biggest pet peeves is men who do not use proper English in messages. It drives me insane. We are too grown for you not to know how to say "Hello, how are you doing?" in a complete sentence. Why are you thirty-five and still dating with no purpose AND no grammar?

I do not have time to play college and early twenties games. I have things to do, bills to pay, boxing classes to attend, and personal growth to attain. My request is this: date with purpose or please leave me alone. In the words on r. h. Sin: "She is evolving, don't distract her."[16] If you are not adding, you are subtracting, and I am not looking to be in the negative.

Dating takes work and effort; it's fueled by the desire to want to be with a person and create something with them. I want the dates, the *I miss yous*, the two-second check-in phone calls because that's all the time you have, the random meetups just because you have some spare time and want to see each other. I like putting energy into someone; it shows them that I value them and their time. Time is one thing, unlike money, you cannot get back. It is very precious to me. I am a "one man at a time" type of girl. This whole "don't put your eggs in one basket" thing, I understand it, but there are better analogies. When I meet a guy, this is not a situation where I am looking for someone to fill a role, so I do not have to accept all the applications.

I get overwhelmed easily, which is why talking to multiple people is not for me. I like to take my time and build a rapport with a person to see if we match. That's why the initial

---

16  r. h. Sin (@rhsin), "she's evolving don't distract her," Instagram photo, July 9, 2019.

process is *yikes*. I feel as though every flaw is on the table and anything I say can go left at any moment. To think I'm going to sit here and do this with two to three people at the same time, absolutely not! That's just asking for me to have a nervous breakdown.

It's probably why Tinder and other dating apps are not the first thing I jump to out there. Some days, it is a means of amusing myself for ten minutes. I told you earlier that apps have corrupted us. I think to myself,

*I am going to lay here and pretend what this could be like. . . Oh, he doesn't like ice cream. NEXT!*

What sort of vetting process is this? I'm entirely too emotional and hopelessly romantic for a world of swiping left and right. What does that mean for me and the wedding I've been planning in my head for the past ten years? I don't know, but I can promise when it does happen though, there will be a candy bar!

In terms of the process of dating itself, I am here for it. I think it offers a lot of lessons about yourself that you could only learn from being with someone. It helps you learn and understand what you want and don't want. It is also a great teacher of compromise. My dad even told me once that it was "healthy," to which I promptly responded (in my head, of course, I have Caribbean/African parents, so even at twenty-seven, I'm not crazy):

*"I don't think this level of stress is healthy for anyone, actually."*

However, his point was directed to what I had mentioned previously on the lessons we learn. I just don't think I would use the word healthy. Informative, maybe, but not healthy.

While most of my dating has been surface level, it taught me that while there are many unanswered questions, I do know what I want. I want something that is real.

When I say that "I want something real," I would be remiss to not ask, what does "real" even look like? I am sure we all have varying definitions, but the underlying concepts are the same. First thoughts: Real to me is someone who is my person, not to sound creepy in a possessive way, but he is mine and I am his. I know I am a priority in their life, and they know the same holds true for them in my life. They are the first person I call with good news, the person I make time for, the person I check in on, and the shoulder I can lean on when things are not going right.

As much as fairytales structure what we grow up to think a relationship should be, I know it's not all good days, but it's also not all bad. Going a level deeper, your person is someone who you still love even when you do not like them at that moment. To the public eye, you are the dynamic duo, and you settle your differences in the privacy of your own home. Full transparency, I know I am a lot when I get upset. I do not get bitchy often, but if pushed, we can fight in the back of the house like grown humans. We are human, so emotions will bubble over. So, fight hard, let it all out, and forgive harder. "Real" is not a destination for finding someone. It is a journey of discovering yourself and this person together, a journey with no end—just the endless discovery of life, laughter, tribulations, and love.

My real-life example is my parents. I hope to have an example like them for my own kids. There are so many stories out there that keep my faith alive. In a submission to *Cosmopolitan Magazine*, a reader wrote, "Friend had been on a flight from London to Australia to go traveling for a few months—she didn't have a full itinerary planned, but roughly knew what she was doing. She was traveling alone, but her seatmate struck up a conversation. They had a great time and found out they'd even studied the same subject at university. They parted ways when they landed in Hong Kong. When they boarded the next flight in Hong Kong, however, they found they were again seated next to each other. Upon landing in Australia, the guy was supposed to go on to New Zealand, but they both decided to ditch their plans, and travel together. They've been together ever since."[17]

Again, I ask, *is this too much to ask for?*

I recognized that dating in this generation was not for me during a conversation with a friend. One day, he and I were talking about the climate of dating right now, and I expressed how I thought it was selfish and inconsiderate of others' feelings. In general, people tend to look for this perfect finished product of an individual in their mind, when in reality, we are all works in progress to different degrees. Also, people want everything to work the way they see fit instead of taking into consideration the other person they are involved with. If the two do not see eye to eye, the individual is ready to jump ship because apparently, "there are so many fish in the seas" that they do not have to put in the effort to even try to compromise. Completing that rant, I thought that it was a shame that it seems so hard to find relationships like what our parents have (his parents have been together for decades now as well). His response was that if I am after what my parents have, there is a strong possibility I could die alone.

---

17  Paisley Gilmour, "13 Ridiculously Cute Stories of How Couples Met to Restore Your Faith in Love," *Cosmopolitan*, October 23, 2017.

There are so many things to unpack here. The first one being *wow*; who tells their best friend they could die alone for actually caring about the type of person they date? We were both fortunate enough to grow up in homes with parents who set good relationship examples, so why can we not also strive toward that model? More importantly, should we not be encouraging each other to strive for the best, find someone who matches your energy, and not settle for the bullshit that people are trying to sell you? The complacency of just accepting the situation as "that is just how it is" is not the answer, and I am not going to stand for that either or allow someone I care about to fall into that trap.

I wish I could skip this whole dating phase and jump straight to "baecations" (vacations with my significant other). There is so much pressure now, with so many "options" out there, that what is one to do to keep themselves as active players? People tell you there are plenty of fish in the sea to make you feel better, but it doesn't lessen my anxiety. Why? Because fish are scary, and they have big eyes just staring at me, waiting for me to mess up. I'm editing every sentence in my head, timing every giggle, trying to remember if I'm arching the right eyebrow because you know... angles. Dating has morphed into a show of proving you are worth something instead of genuinely trying to get to know someone.

Yeah, twenty-first-century dating is soooo not for me. But I am in it, and if there's one thing Nicole McKenzie is not, that's a quitter. I still believe in real love, and that's the spark that keeps me going. It's not like the love of my life is going to be my Uber Eats delivery driver. But hey, who knows?

# "I'VE BEEN SINGLE SO LONG, I FEEL LIKE I'M ON YEAR-END CLEARANCE"

---

Today is July 27, 2020, and earlier today as I was casually scrolling through my Instagram timeline minding my own business, I was witness to another engagement. Honestly, I could not have asked for a better setup or segue to address this chapter and these annoying things we call "feelings."

My initial thought is filled with love, joy, and lots of hand claps.

"Yes, girl, I am here for all the Black love and joy."

After scrolling for a few more minutes, I clicked off and sat back in my chair. My mind wandered to the engagement again. Again, I am hit with a wave of joy for them, but after a few seconds, there is a change in the emotional tide. I go from joy that slowly dissipates into a feeling of disbelief, followed by disappointment that just settled. No, I was not being petty toward her. Her engagement was beautiful, and I admit there were tears.

The negativity was toward myself, which brings us to thought number two:

"It has to be me, because there is no way."

Have you ever been really excited and then, five seconds later, heartbroken? If you have, then you know what I am talking about it. If you have not, I 10/10 do not ever recommend going through those emotions together, because all it does is confuse you.

We are going to talk about looking for love, and I know I will the audacity to agree with those people who tell us, "It will happen when you least expect it." So, why on Earth would I title the chapter before, "I've Been Single so Long, I Feel like I'm on Year-End Clearance"?

In the words of my girl Angelica, "It has to be the crack." No, no it's not. It is Instagram! It is alllll Instagram's fault. Dammit, and we were doing so well.

I am a strong, independent woman: I have a job, I pay my own bills, and my skin care routine right now is unparalleled. My melanin is popping in this nonexistent summer of 2020. So, why is the first thought I directed to myself, "What is wrong with me?" Seriously, what the fuck?

It's almost ironic I decided to pen this chapter on this day, because earlier in the day, before I saw the engagement post, I came across a tweet posted by @idontdoclubs, and the tweet comes from Kaya Nova, "I noticed when I tell people about dating issues they immediately say 'but you're so amazing! Your person is coming or you're so beautiful, its gonna happen!' And I just have to ask since when have women being amazing or beautiful guaranteed us a safe, fulfilled dating life?"[18]

I have never had a statement resonate with me as much as this had. She is not wrong; I know what I bring to the table, and of course that doesn't mean someone will sit down, but even if they do, is it company that will last?

Society has built this construct around us, claiming that our lovely personality and our "damn girl, you a ten" looks are supposed to be our golden ticket into a fulfilling dating life. I call bullshit, because isn't this the same society that makes us feel crazy for not having a fulfilling relationship, a ring on our finger by twenty-four, kids, and a white-picket-fence house by twenty-eight (potentially being on kid number two by thirty, depending on how you spread your births out)? Dear society, if that was all I needed to be successful, why am I not living up to your expectations?

When I was in high school, I always thought I would be married by twenty-five, having kids by twenty-eight, and breaking ground on my dream home by thirty. Well, I turn twenty-eight March 2021, and you know what I don't have? A boyfriend, let alone being on track anywhere close to having kids—and do not get me started on my lease agreement.

I feel as though I am in a battle with myself. The current me versus the me I think I should be.

People will ask, "How are you doing?" I have constantly said, "Trying to get my life together." Does anyone ever fully *get* their life *together*? Isn't the whole point of life

---

18  Kaya Nova (@thekayanova) "I noticed when I tell people about dating issues they immediately say "but you're so amazing! Your person is coming or you're so beautiful, its gonna happen!" And I just have to ask since when have women being amazing or beautiful guaranteed us a safe, fulfilled dating life?" Twitter, June 29, 2020, 3:57 p.m.

adapting to change and enjoying the moments? I stop and wonder if other people ever feel like they are behind. We talked about this earlier, when all your family and relatives are asking, "When are you going to get married?" It's almost like you missed a milestone you didn't know you were supposed to reach. Admittedly at times, I have felt like I have failed at something. I am super single, with no prospects, and am entirely too invested in *Bridgerton*.

On the flip side, I stop my downward spiral and think, is it me, or is it actually society? Like, dear people who created these constructs, i.e. mostly men, are you afraid of what women can do on their own? Is that why you start throwing shade at the age of twenty-five? Because if we all tapped into the power we all possess, you would be screwed. I am just asking for a friend.

It has gotten to this point though, where my idealistic views are really at war with one another. When I sit and think about it, there is not anything inherently wrong with my reality. We all have our own struggles. I am healthy, I have a job, I have great friends. I am learning new things, accomplishing things I never thought I would, including writing this book, and just taking life as it is. Dear society, what is so wrong with that?

I have had to learn to talk myself down from the ledge when my idealism of relationships coupled with society starts knocking. Honestly, tapping into my spirituality has helped a lot, too. Regardless of your beliefs and/or where you are in your journey, I do believe we all have our own path in this life, each one unique to each individual.

Society has unfortunately tainted us with the belief that we are all on similar paths with the same objective goals such as school, a career, a home, and a relationship. However, the fact of the matter is, we may all have similar goals, but no one is on the same trajectory—and most definitely not the same timeline.

That was how I broke the chains of pressure. This is my life. Steph Curry said once in an interview that the best advice his mom ever gave him was, "No one gets to write your story but you."

No one gets to tell me when I should be married. When the right guy comes along, it will happen. I'm looking for THE right relationship, not the right NOW relationship.

No one gets to tell me when I should have kids. I will when I am damn ready!

No one gets to tell me that I can't [insert whatever societal pressure you feel]. It's your life, it's my life. We get to write the story.

My friends are married! This is amazing because I love weddings. Others are having kids. Phenomenal, because I love clothes shopping for babies. They are buying homes. Fantastic, I can't wait to see their kitchens.

This is a battle society is not going to win. I am not going to settle for less than I deserve to make people who do not even know me judge me less because I am finally on "their" appropriate timeline.

If Prince Charming shows up at thirty, he shows up at thirty. If Logan (yes, I have baby names) isn't born until thirty-three, she is born at thirty-three. If the five-bedroom, 5.5-bath, two-story home with the sprawling backyard and pool doesn't get purchased until thirty-five, I sign on the dotted line at thirty-five. If any of these events happen in a reverse order, then they happen as they may.

Until the time is right, I will be babysitting, screaming over engagements, hitting these gym goals, partying at these weddings, brunching like a habit, and flourishing like a fun-sized pack of M&Ms. Period!

End Quote: "If you find yourself constantly trying to prove your worth to someone, you have already forgotten your value."[19]

---

19 "If You Find Yourself Constantly Trying to Prove Your Worth to Someone, You Have Already Forgotten Your Value," *Tiny Buddha*, last modified June 9, 2015.

# PART III

# HOW DATING WORKS IF YOU ARE GOING TO DO IT?

# PART III

# HOW DATING WORKS IF YOU ARE GOING TO DO IT?

# LOOKING FOR LOVE

—

*Relatable Tweet: @emmabetsinger: There's plenty of fish in the sea but know what else there is? Trash. There is a lot of trash in the sea.*[20]

Does this phrase sound familiar to all the single folks in the room?

"Don't look for love, it'll happen when you least expect it."

That phrase is the premise of every romantic comedy ever written. One of my personal favorites is *27 Dresses*. For those of you who haven't seen it, the premise is pretty simple: "always a bridesmaid and never a bride." Who would have thought, the guy who started out on a mission to write a pretty hurtful story about Jane being a perpetual bridesmaid would learn there are layers to her and end up falling for her?

*Answer:* anyone who pressed play on this movie. It's a romantic comedy, so *of course* things were going to work out.

I know movies are fiction, so is this overused phrase really supposed to apply to real life?

---

20  Pedro Fequiere, "Twenty-one Times Animals Proved to Be The Best Things on the Internet," *Buzzfeed,* July 13, 2018.

This is by far one of my favorite things to hear. . .

Do you sense the sarcasm?

Nothing drives people like me up the wall more than this sentence. It's like a bad recording that you can't shut off because it's coming from all sides. I want to take a microphone and scream, "I GET IT." However, I do refrain from such antics because that would be rude. I know folks are just trying to help.

The root of this statement is the premise that the best things in life happen when you least expect them to happen, which is, for the most part, true. Finding love shouldn't be like finding the city of gold. We should not have to become Nicholas Cage in *National Treasure* to find a partner, stealing artifacts to find hidden codes and directions. Yes, we should make ourselves available, but we shouldn't be mentally and physically exhausted by it. When the relationship actually starts—now, that requires work, even though people think it doesn't. However, that is an explanation for another time.

For many it does; relationships do tend to fall into people's laps when they least expect it. One awesome young lady I interviewed is a perfect example of this.

She and I shared our experiences when it came to dating apps. Much like the rest of us, it was not her cup of tea. Weird conversations, bad dates, the whole package of dating app scares. The day she was ready to call it quits, she matched with this guy. Not expecting much, she decided to indulge him and strike up a conversation. Turns out, she had finally caught herself a fish and not a Styrofoam cup. They just celebrated their two-year anniversary (shout out to them for showing us apps aren't all bad, just bad a solid 92 percent of the time).

While I agree with the spontaneity of meeting someone, contrary to popular belief, it does involve a bit of work. That work is making yourself available, meaning, going outside and being among people. Unless you are one of the lucky few meeting your future partner in a place you frequent already, you do have to venture out some. That is, if you are looking to meet someone organically the way our parents talk about. Buses, grocery stores, trains, clubs, and airports are all viable options, but they also require pants, shoes, and a smile that's plastered on in the hopes that someone looks your way.

On the other hand, if the apps are more what you are involved in, that is going to take more hands-on work, because Tinder doesn't swipe itself and Hinge cannot hit "yes" to a match for you.

I know I am being very nit-picky about this phrase, and people tend to not make it this literal, but I still think the point should be addressed. The key here is accessibility. I tend to be a homebody, so unless the Uber Eats guy is going to be the love of my life, I am a little screwed. However, because of COVID, Uber Eats doesn't even deliver to your door, they just drop it off, so even that slim possibility is gone.

In my life right now, there are so many moving parts, and the idea of swiping every day through trash bags until I find a good piece of salmon sounds like just too much work entirely, but I admit there is a bit of longing. I have nights where I swipe with hope and open-mindedness, but about fifteen minutes later, I'm over it. By the time this book publishes, I will be in my late twenties, and I am at the point in my life where friends and acquaintances are building serious relationships, getting a ring on it, walking down the aisle, and birthing children. All the while, I am sitting in my apartment with my Netflix and Tonight Dough.

People who love you tend to think the world of you. They know the good, the bad, the ugly, and the crazy but still see the value in you. They feel there is someone out there who will see that and so much more in you. You and your future partner will have ups and downs, but you will also have straight Rihanna vibes and shine like a Fenty Gloss Bomb. At that moment when your friends are hyping you up, you soak it all up. Then you start hyping yourself up like, "Yeah, I am that queen!"

However, a few weeks after this positivity is shot, reality hits. You find yourself in a space alone, and your mind begins to wander. It's at this moment that the future you see and the future your friends see are two different places.

Friendly reminder: this is not a constant space. It can happen when someone you thought you were having a good conversation with decides to unmatch with you, silencing you in the middle of a thought. It can happen when you've had the longest day, and all you want to do is curl up with your person, the one who understands you and loves you. It happened to me the night I edited this chapter for the first time. It took a pep talk to bring myself out of my feelings. Many a time, I try to downplay my feelings to myself by saying they don't matter, but the truth is it does. I think it's important to allow ourselves to feel so we don't become overwhelmed.

I am the queen of bottling up my emotions, which is ironic given how much I value emotional expression. I bottle mine up more for conformity reasons, but that isn't the point here. Speaking of someone unmatching you, recently I had an experience with a lovely young man. He and I matched and had an amazing conversation. We talked about everything and nothing at the same time. Turns out, he was in a bit of a situation. I just felt like the biggest idiot, like I was robbed in a sense. Intellectual compatibility for me is a must but so hard to come by that when it happens, I treasure it. In that moment, I felt like the universe had set me up to fail—and this is the same universe that has me waiting for my unexpected. I am going to need the universe to do better. In the same breath, I tried to pretend that not being able to talk to him didn't affect me. It was whatever until I went to work a few days later, and all I could envision for fifteen minutes was destroying an entire shelf of product just to dissipate this pent-up rage that started as a simmer that I was not even aware of.

It's normal to want to feel wanted and loved. Meeting someone and being able to engage with them is the first step to this journey. It sucks when it seems you cannot even launch past "hello."

Usually, right after "It'll happen when you least expect it" is where people tend to insert the "Just be patient, you have time." I have a very real question: what do you think I'm doing right now?

Just because I say I want to date someone or be in a relationship does not mean that is my only focus. I am not actively looking for a partner. I am more passively keeping my eyes open.

My friends have been telling me for years, "It'll happen. The future awaits." Question: when exactly is this "future"? Like, are we talking five years? Ten? Twenty? Am I going to end up dead before "it'll happen" kicks in? (I'm very aware that this is a little dramatic, but bear with me.) In the seemingly never-ending road of statements such as "your person will pop up soon," I just don't know when it's going to happen. I recognize that I am not supposed to know, but come on, cut me some slack. I have witnessed probably close to ten engagements in the last year, and all I want right now is someone not to stand me up.

Plus, do you ever notice that the people telling you to be patient are all people who are in a relationship? I am waiting for the punchline. I have a super chill friend, Anthony, who is a married service man. Despite his marital status, women still shamelessly throw themselves at him. Don't we all love a man in uniform? Our friendship is several years strong, and he is my go-to when I need a male opinion. It's a good thing I love him so much, because while some of his responses are really useful, some make me question why I thought to ask him to begin with.

One day, I was venting my frustrations to him and he responded very nonchalantly:

"I don't understand why you let all this stress you out."

I screamed out loud—and not a little squeak like you would do when a squirrel unexpectedly runs past. No, a full-blown "I have four years of pent-up frustration to express in this one minute" type of scream. Excuse me, sir, am I not allowed to feel my own emotions for a moment before you try and downplay my experiences and frustrations?

After I calmed down about ninety seconds later, I told him quite pointedly, "You do not know what it is like for me, you don't even know what it's like to be dating right now in general. You and your wife have been married for six years, you have been together for like twelve years now, and you still got women throwing themselves at you left, right, and center. You are constantly being validated. You don't know what it feels like to be me. To feel like no matter how hard you try, it's not going to work."

"Of course, you don't understand what I'm going through. You have someone to go home to at night. I'm just trying to find someone to go to brunch with."

He was a little taken aback at first, but he did finally understand my point. That is all I am looking for; I just want a little understanding from the folks who have traversed to the other side of the dating game.

To all the booed-up friends trying to encourage their single friends who may lean a bit more on the emotional side, my advice is to let them vent. Before you go headfirst into the pep talk of, "Don't feel that way, it'll happen for you," I'm begging you to stop yourself, please.

Chances are, you have already told them the above statement a few times. They remember, trust me. It can make their feelings feel invalid. It puts salt on the wound, reiterating the fact that this was not the halibut one was looking for but just a piece of plastic floating around the dating pool. I know this isn't your intention, but it comes off as, "Oh, you shouldn't feel that way because something will happen in the future." The keyword here is "future," but what about right now? What about what this person is feeling in this moment? That's what they are working through, not the future you are wishing for them.

Instead, just hear them out. They just need an outlet to vent their frustration. Let them get it all the way out, and then give them a hug or a bottle of wine. Honestly, the two are a great combo.

Just spend some time with them. When the ranting has stopped, just talk about anything. The weather, the sale Sephora had, talk about that one person you both don't like and how her lace was showing. (I know, I know, rude, but it made you laugh because you thought about that one person you and your friends always talk shit about—none of you are immune.)

To my single, ready-to-mingle folks. I hate to betray you like this, but it probably will happen when you least expect it. My hope for you and me is that your special someone is able to match that impeccable energy you exude. When that feeling of singleness washes over you, don't try and force it away. Pause, acknowledge it, feel it, and then put it away. Remember, "You are nobody's plan B, either they choose you or lose you."[21]

---

21  sWooZie (@sWooZie), "I Ain't Nobodys Plan B. Either You Choose Me or You Lose Me," Twitter, September 11, 2012, 5:58 p.m.

# THE APPS

—

I want to first dedicate this chapter to the person who gave me the idea of this book: Alexa. She and I have never bonded harder than we did on this topic right here.

Where do we find people to date? Before 1995, you had to meet people in person. Your friends would set you up, your family would invite a friend, you could meet someone on the bus, the grocery store, wherever—the possibilities were endless. Dating was an all-human interaction without an interface. Then in 1995, we got our first online dating service, Match.com, but I doubt back then people thought online dating would evolve into what it is now. We have come a long way from the days of Match. Now, it's not even a ".com"; we just have apps for days.

Most people who know me know that I am old-fashioned and still holding out to meet someone organically, and to have a fun story to tell my kids, the way my parents did. However, I am in a trifecta of pickles. When I go out, I feel invisible and transform into a wallflower. Contrarily, I am always so busy, I live in three places: my house, work, and the gym. Finally, the fact that people don't talk anymore, communicating solely on their phones, makes online dating seem like a requirement.

As bothersome as I find online dating, it's not a shock that it has become so popular. It cuts out half the work of having to be approachable. It's easy to hide behind a screen when your personality is one that is subject to the individual you "meet."

Let's say for once, I have a free weekend and decide I am going to leave the comforts of my apartment. I am an introverted extrovert. Sometimes I get hit with the social bug and will get my nails done, tame my edges, dig for my heels, and says yes to invites of going out. Most nights, I would like to be in my oversized T-shirt, curled up in a blanket watching either basketball or football, depending on the season. However, I would like to get married one day, so sometimes I have to suck it up and pull on the Spanx.

But this night is the night of yes. Got dolled up. Pulled out your heels. Shaved your legs. Arched your eyebrows. The highlighter is popping. Edges are laid. Just all types of Yasss Queen vibes. IG stories are lit. I have had enough shots that I actually believe I'll survive in those 4.5-inch stilettos, and out the door I go. In my head, I am ready for a girls' night. It'll be great, but in the back, back, back of your mind you think maybe there'll be someone cute to look at. We all appreciate a little eye candy.

Bar, lounge, club, wherever the music is right, that's where you are tonight. The drinks are flowing, and I feel amazing, enjoying the night with your girls. One, or a group of guys, will approach, and they will start talking to everyone except me, because you know they have their eyes on a prize. They will be chatting up one friend while being casually friendly to the other.

Sidebar: we can tell the difference between you trying to talk to me and you trying to "talk to me." Ninety-nine percent of the time, it's always the former when you slow-stroll up to a group of women and try to insert yourself into a place where you are unfamiliar.

Stuff like this, where my friends get approached and I am invisible, has happened in many places. The club, the street (I have seen a man break his neck trying to turn around and talk to my friend waiting on an Uber.)—name a situation, I have probably been a wallflower to it.

The truth is, I am not even mad at the situation. My friends are 10/10s, so I expect that. Also, I am not even mad at him, because that is his preference. It's just, sometimes I can't help but wonder, "Is it me?"

· Is it something I said?
· Is it the way I look?
· The way I dressed?
· What is it about me?

It's always the questions that seep into my mind. Logically, I know that this line of questioning doesn't make sense. However, I have learned that if you see a pattern, look for the common denominator; that's what the pattern is. If I am the common denominator, where else would my mind go?

This is not exclusive to physical spaces. I actually think online dating and sliding into DMs have made this just so much more exaggerated.

Since we are living predominantly in a digital world, we are going to focus on that. Introducing the online dating websites and the ever-evolving dating apps. I think it's important to first introduce some of the players. There are over one thousand five hundred dating sites/apps, but I'm not going to list them all, don't worry. Marisa Lascala gives the best description of these apps:

"Tinder: For those trying to cast the widest net

Bumble: Ladies, if you want to make the first move

Plenty of Fish (POF): For daters just out of college (eh. I have a few things to say about this one)

Happn: If you're looking for a guy (explanation: according to its data there are more men downloading the app than women so the ratio works in your favor hun!)

Grindr: For LGBTQ Daters

Coffee Meets Bagel: For those who need a little push (explanation: the app offers icebreaking prompts and gentle reminders to respond to your waiting messages.)

Ship: For people who can't make decisions (explanation: Ship lets your friends weigh in and vet your matches. That way, if your date is a bust, you can spread the blame around.)

Hinge: For people who are over Tinder"[22]

There is one that I have used that didn't make the *Good Housekeeping* list and that is The League: it is considered an "elite dating app" where you have to apply to get access. Your job title and the college you attended are factors in your application process. The waitlist is hundreds of people long. I thought this was a platform to meet new people, not a job application.

We have the apps and, if you're into sliding into people's DMs, the joys of Instagram. Not for nothing, I didn't realize how big of a thing this was until someone told me her friend's IG has more DMs than her phone has texts. People are really out here shooting their shot—just not with me.

---

22  Marisa LaScala. "If You're Sick of Being Single, It's Time to Download a New Dating App," *Good Housekeeping,* July 17, 2020.

I have swiped, I have liked, and I have written many hellos, and I swear I get stuck with all the crazies or folks who lack basic common sense. For example, you guys can think I'm wrong for this all you want, but there was a guy I matched with, and this was our conversation:

"Where are you from?"

"Guyana"

"Where is that at?"

I indulged because apparently, my country was left out of geography class for many.

"It's in South America, but it is considered part of the Caribbean"

"Yea, I think I heard of it. Y'all like Nigerian music, right?"

With the invention of Google, I am sorry, but no. I'm not, nope. Seriously, even geographically that doesn't make sense. I get that DJs like to play Caribbean music and Afrobeats at parties, but please. . . Please, I'm just asking for a break.

I promise you this is not an isolated case. There are people embarking on phenomenal dates, in relationships for years, getting married, and I am can't even have a decent conversation. This book is all about being open and putting myself out there. For anyone who may think I'm overreacting, in 2019 I was asked out on three dates and subsequently got stood up for all three. I am a drama queen sometimes, but I usually have the receipts to back up my statements.

Dating apps have taught me some things and highlighted a few others. I think I remember when dating apps started popping up, they were slowly evolving from this weird thing that people did, into something that was on its way to being mainstream.

My first app was OkCupid, the predecessor to Tinder.

In the beginning, I was hesitant. In a way I think I felt embarrassed that in a whole university and all the intermingling activities, there wasn't even one inkling of potential, so I had to step into this completely foreign world. However, I had spent almost three years in college at this point with no play in my life, so I figured, why not. It was a pretty fast trial run, though. OkCupid and I were a bust, but we broke up on amicable terms.

I feel like OkCupid is still popping, but I don't know for who because they have real ads, not just the stuff that pops up on your sponsored IG ads because the government is watching. I have been in the Metro station in Washington, DC, and seen full-blown electronic posters. I guess on the flip side, I have also seen full e-poster adds for Grindr on the Metro, so to each their own.

Next, I ventured along to POF, and while that eventually ended in divorce, there was a light at the end of the tunnel, and honey, he was fine. Alas, we were young and went our separate ways. If you guessed that I am referring to Kenny, you are correct. More champagne for everyone!

Out of curiosity, I tried Tinder, and that was a swipe to the left. I had some guy I matched with years back when I was less jaded ask me if I really thought I was going to find someone on Tinder since everything is based on superficial information. While his observation was not wrong, he still did not need to call my naïveté out like that.

Does anyone else sometimes feel like they are now drowning in options? When did the App Store become this popping with dating apps? It comes with all different levels and ranges. Like, why is there one just for Vegans and Yogis, like do I have to be 100 percent committed to these two things to join? What if I'm vegan and not a yogi but have no problem dating a yogi? Are you going to judge me for lack of a meditation schedule?

Even celebrities have their own. There is an app called Raya, which is supposed to be for "celebrities." You have to be invited by someone already on the app, or you get waitlisted to be approved to enter. Nicole Byer talks about it a lot on her podcast. She was waitlisted for two years. Dear dating app developers and associates, y'all are not serious. It is never that deep, especially because in apps like Raya and The League, these people also have Hinge and Tinder profiles. There are loopholes to your exclusivity. No one has just one app.

I have done the message first with Bumble and appreciated the men who actually took time to fill out their Hinge profiles. Nothing has been a real match. Just a whole lot of introductions and disappearances. Got to love a good ghost.

Now, Hinge and Bumble are my go-tos. Even finally committing to an app where I think there is potential brings a whole new onslaught of problems.

How do I present myself? Where do I draw the line between providing just enough information to seem interesting and approachable, and too much information that there is no way in hell anyone is going to read all of that? When completing your profile, I wonder, how do I translate who I am digitally? In-person I can give you a 10/10 presentation on Nicole McKenzie, but online I feel like I never get it right.

Then you have to think about the safety concerns. Online dating is truly a leap of faith in folks. That is why I always recommend a FaceTime call before you ever meet anyone. Make sure those pictures match up because identity thieves have moved past just social security numbers. If *Catfish* has taught us something, it is to be very aware of who we are talking to.

Once we pass the interface itself, we get to us. The people behind the screen. Each app has been created to facilitate the answer to this fundamental question. Ladies and gentlemen, "What do we want?"

Are we looking for commitment or a hookup?

Your go could be Tinder.

Do we want the label or just someone to vibe with?

Your go could be Bumble or Coffee Meets Bagel.

I am at this place in my life where the amount of married people I know and those with kids is making me start to think a little harder about myself. I want that, I want to meet someone with good intentions, and I want that meeting to lead to commitment and progress into a 14K Rose Gold Luxe Viviana Diamond Engagement ring. Eventually evolving into a beautiful home and two to three babies.

I know I should not compare my experiences and journey to someone else's. God has put us each on our own timeline. Sometimes, though, that pep talk gets a little annoying. I think we should all be allowed the grace to feel frustrated for a few minutes, to let it go, and to regroup.

During our stay-at-home orders in early 2020, I was flipping through my IG stories casually one morning, doing more tapping than actually watching. I got to one story that made me pause and two subsequent ones that caused me to fully stop. All three of the stories included people whose significant others had made them dinner. One couple was dating, the other couple was married, and the last was engaged. I'll be honest, I raised my eyebrow a bit, looking at my self-made boiled eggs thinking, this is not even right, I had to cook my own dinner last night. I mean, come on, three in a row? Isn't the IG algorithm supposed to be better than this? I want someone to make my food; I'll cook for you in return!

One: food is totally one of the keys to my heart, and two: I hate cooking for just myself. It's a lot of work for absolutely no reason, and I actually enjoy cooking. It just makes me beg the question sometimes of . . .

"You know, let's not go there."

I am on the apps both willingly and unwillingly. I know that if I want it to work, I have to try and not be bored after five minutes. Part of me is still holding out hope for my organic meeting. Until then, I will give the likes and swipes a chance. For those of you still going, keep on swiping on. I hope you find what you are looking for. . . eventually. You know, the apps have brought us so much: options, fun men, crazy men, wild men, and, my personal favorite, ghosting men.

# GHOSTING

———

It has been about two weeks since you last heard from him. For some reason, you are still desperately staring at your screen attempting to will a text into existence. Honey, I hate to break it to you, but I think you have been ghosted.

I believe communication to be a better response than ghosting. However, there are a few instances when ghosting is necessary. The most important aspect of ghosting is safety. Sometimes people cannot take a hint. This happens to both men and women alike. However, for a woman, a man who won't stop trying to talk to you could pose a safety issue. For example, if he keeps texting you "good morning," and his text thread just looks like he is having a conversation with himself, you can move on to level two ghosting and just block his ass.

Hey Siri, define ghosting: "When a person cuts off all communication with their friends or the person they're dating, with zero warning or notice beforehand. You'll mostly see them avoiding friends' phone calls, social media, and avoiding them in public."[23]

———

23  *Urban Dictionary*, s.v. "ghosting," accessed August 19, 2020.

I am not going to sit here and front like I have not ghosted someone. Sometimes, the easy option wins over the right option. I am trash! I know. At least I can admit when I am being trash, unlike some people I know.

In the times I have participated in ghosting, it has usually occurred in the first few days or the first week of me talking to them. I do not ghost people after I have been talking to them for weeks/months. By that point, you start to build connections and experiences together. They are no longer just some strangers in your life that you just met.

Ghosting does not just apply to dating; it can happen with anyone in your life. The time frames of ghosting can be as confusing as the reasons. They may have stepped out for a few weeks, or they may have packed all their stuff in the middle of the night and left your life forever. Besides the fact that I hate ghosting in general, I get irrationally angry about people who "soft ghost you," which I will dive into later on in this chapter. Some of you might want to find a seat because this is a very touchy subject for me.

I am going to make a PSA: When I say men, I don't mean all men. I do have some amazing men in my life who deserve credit. I know there are still amazing men out there. In this chapter, "men" will be referring to the men who only open their mouths in their own self-interest.

Ghosting as a general phenomenon is not something new. We just revamped the technique in the digital age. As Megan Murray from *Stylist Magazine* writes, "Before online dating was a thing, our parents called this being strung along."[24]

---

24  Megan Murray, "Have You Been Soft Ghosted in the Age of Virtual Dating? Here's How to Tell," *Stylist*, December 29, 2020.

Why do people ghost? The person who did the ghosting assumingly did it because they do not want to talk to whoever they ghosted. The person who has been ghosted likely doesn't think highly of the person doing the ghosting. They could have just said something instead of throwing up their peace sign and walking out.

In my life, I have personally been ghosted for two reasons.
1. I do not know.
2. Lack of communication.

When Damien (I will explain who he is very soon) and I were "together," I learned he was one of those people who didn't like to talk through their feelings. He just liked to keep it inside and sort it out himself. I respected that, everyone is entitled to deal with and reflect on difficult situations in their own way. However, when he would have these moments, he would disappear off the face of my side of the planet while still being active in other parts. It would drive me absolutely crazy.

I do not do well with silence. I am inherently a fixer, so I want everything to be good and happy. Random silence ruins that for me. I addressed this behavior with him, and I was honest.

I told him, "I understand you need time for yourself. However, it's also not fair for you to disappear without a trace. You won't respond to anything I say, but you seem to have the time and ability to be posting on Snapchat and Instagram as though everything is fine and dandy. Not only do I feel disrespected, but I feel hurt as well."

All I was looking for from him was an open line of communication. If you do not want to talk, that is 100 percent ok, just say that. If something is going on, you don't have to explain it to me. All it takes is one sentence: "Hey, I don't want to talk, and I just need this time to myself." Done! You and I don't have any problems, this is open communication, you have your time and space, and I am aware of the vibes and energy of the space we are in together.

Damien would sometimes get confused about why I reacted the way I did to his silence. Then, I was confused about why he was confused.

Everyone is different, so how we handle and perceive situations is going to be different. This is my perspective: if I am in a relationship, situationship, entanglement, or whatever with someone and something happens and you just up and stop talking to me with no explanation for days on end, then we have a problem because you left the sentence as a fragment. What am I supposed to think? This is how assumptions start and how misunderstandings develop.

Finally, when he had worked though his emotions and was calm enough to re-enter the world we shared, he had the audacity to be "confused" as to why I was mad. Admittedly, I had a bit of an attitude when he came back, but wouldn't you? Now, he is mad at my attitude, which now progresses me to be second-degree mad about how he has the audacity to think I have no right to feel some type of way because he left me at the table alone. All of this aggression, confusion, and misunderstanding bubbles into a fight for grand proportions that could have been avoided with five words.

Now, I have a whole essay for you with an introduction, three supporting paragraphs, and a conclusion about why you are wrong. Seriously, this is not rocket science.

Honestly, part of it from my experience is as a culture and generation, we have gotten so caught up in this "it's all about me, I'm going to do me, nobody is going to have an effect on me" mentality that we forget that we still have people in our lives to consider. If you are in any type of relationship (friendships count too as they are a type of relationship), you are in a partnership of some sort with another person, which means you have to be considerate of each other. There is a difference between having self-care and just being straight-up selfish, you know?

Ghosting, I feel, has gotten completely out of control since dating apps became so popular. It's like we have the attention span of a five-year-old. When this one isn't shiny and new anymore, we drop it for something else.

While I don't approve of ghosting at all, I have participated in it. This dating app world is a little frightening, and sometimes it's easier to just stop responding. I'll admit, I think ghosting is ok within the app. If you and this person have pulled your conversation out of the app, you have reached the borderline territory. If you have set up a date and never show up, that is a violation of respect rules, and any ghosting after the second date is just rude.

Suppose you have been chatting to someone for a while and the vibes are good, and now, you are finally ready to meet this person. If you ask a girl on a date and never show up for the date or go radio silent on the day of the date, then you sir, are an ass. You asked her out! Why even bother making plans if you weren't going to follow through!

The sad part is that this has happened to me three times now.

There was Chad, who I met on Hinge. We did the usual chatting: *Tell me about yourself. What do you like to do? How has your week been?* All the boring stuff I keep wishing I could skip over. We chatted for a while on the app, then he asked for my number. We moved to actual texting, and we would even FaceTime sometimes. Then, he asked me if I wanted to go out soon.

At the time, I was in Chicago for work, so I agreed to the weekend after I returned. We kept in touch the week I was in Chicago and would talk every night after I got off of work. The day of the proposed date was when things went very wrong. I had worked at the bakery in the morning, and we had agreed to have dinner at the Harbor.

In the morning, I reached out just to confirm that we were all set. An hour passed, then two, then three, four hours later I had still heard nothing. My shift ended, and while I was disappointed, there was nothing I could do but wait. So, I left work and went to get my nails done. Not even five minutes into my pedicure, he finally responds six hours later. Since I was mid-pedicure, I asked him if we could push back dinner an hour since I was not home yet. He agreed.

I got home, showered, and reached out before I started getting dressed. I had this inkling that this date was not going to happen, and I turned out to be right. He never responded that night or any day after that. However, about a week later he popped up in the most bizarre way. I posted this meme on my Snapchat story that said, "The next person who breaks my heart is getting tased. Oh, look now we are both shocked." This man had the audacity to comment on my post, "I agree." I'm sorry but sir what? It has to be the crack—there is no other explanation. I did not even dignify that with a response.

There was also this other guy, whose name I do not remember, but I remember our lack of encounters. The way he stood me up for our date was truly unmatched. He and I met on POF. We messaged back and forth. FaceTimed with each other almost every day. I enjoyed getting to know him and was thrilled when he asked me out. I was very excited because he was quite a cutie on campus. The evening arrived, and he asked for my address because he offered to pick me up. I got dressed, and took the time to style my hair and perfect all the layers of all my Fenty Beauty products. I put on the finishing touches and called him to see how far away he was. Nothing.

I sent him a text. Nothing.

I tried reaching out one more time, and his text bubbles had gone green.

In a final damsel in distress attempt, I called from the landline in the lobby, and the phone said the number "cannot be reached at this time." Literally, one minute he existed, the next he was gone, and I never quite found out what happened.

There is one more story, but I do not think I could depress myself any further than this. I am like 0/3 when it comes to the execution of a first date. I am so not winning. . .

*I need some champagne, like a whole bottle after reliving all that.*

You know what else I hate about people who ghost? Those who won't just commit to it. Those people who soft ghost you. Soft ghosting refers to someone "liking" your last message or latest comment on their post on platforms like Facebook and Instagram, where it's possible to react to an interaction, but not actually replying and continuing the conversation. So, although they're not ignoring you, they're also offering no genuine response.[25]

Excuse my language but THIS SHIT DRIVES ME CRAZY! If you are going to stop talking to me, go all the

---

25   Megan Murray, "Have You Been Soft Ghosted in the Age of Virtual Dating? Here's How to Tell," *Stylist*, December 29, 2020.

way. Do not half-ass your exit, the way you wanted to half-ass this relationship!

Ok, I am done now.

I think having your best friend, or any friend for that matter, ghost you is actually worse than any person you are romantically involved with because there is actually real history there and love that was shared. For me, it was a proverbial slap in the face; like damn, no one is loyal anymore. This also occurred around the time Damien and I were really, really breaking up. In my head, I was questioning why it seemed as though all of the men in my life were losing their minds all at the same damn time. I was so heated, I almost hit the delete button on all those friendships.

Terrence and I have a long-standing friendship. I have known Terrence since high school. We have been through good times in our friendship, dinners, laughs, even him coming out to see me. We have made it through the rough patches of his ex-girlfriend. Where there was a will, there was a way for us to keep going.

I tell you guys, even though I am confused and mad at him now, I still love the kid. If he called me now, I would answer. I would have some very strongly worded questions, but I would answer.

Back in December 2020, I decided that this year I would get Terrance a gift. He had been looking out for me for a while. He sent me money to get a nice dinner, and he paid for my nails on my birthday, so I wanted to return the favor of generosity. The thing about Terrance is, he is horrendous at answering text messages, so I usually have to call him if I need to talk to him. The negative to that is, I'm always at work, so it becomes a catch-22.

I called him one night asking him what his pant size was because I was planning on getting him some things from Nike. He told me he would get back to me in the morning. He has been radio silent ever since, and that was about six weeks ago.

I have gone over our last conversation in my head countless times trying to find a reason. Honestly, I do not think one exists. To add insult to injury, he has been soft ghosting me. So, while he won't return my calls, he is catching glimpses of my stories. This behavior confuses the hell out of me.

It all boils down to communication. It doesn't have to be active, just keep the lines open. We could save ourselves so much pain, confusion, and disappointment if we would all just learn to talk to one another and be honest. It is something I am working on myself. It is a constant work in progress. Relationships take work, but they are also a constant work in progress. No one is in a relationship alone. It can't be all about you, and if it is, you'll find yourself alone. I know it may not seem like much, but a little consideration and a five-word text can go a very long way.

# CAN MEN AND WOMEN JUST BE FRIENDS?

---

"He isn't my boyfriend, but he still mines."[26]

In telling my story and addressing my specific ups and downs with dating, it wouldn't be right if I didn't talk about that almighty question: "Can men and women just be friends?" There are endless movies and shows where the guy and girl are besties, but one is secretly in love with the other and hates their current significant other. Many rom coms have this plotline; others are more along the *27 Dresses* line, as I mentioned earlier. The movie progresses to the climax where they confess their feelings and live happily ever after. **THE END.**

There are also real-life stories of best friends falling in love, such as Matt Grodsky and Laura Scheel. About twenty years ago, three-year-old Matt Grodsky stood up in front of his entire preschool class in Phoenix, Arizona, declaring that

---

26 Mollie Celine, "I Know He's Not My Boyfriend - but He's Still Mine.: Tagalog Love Quotes, He's Mine Quotes, Back off Quotes." Pinterest, January 23, 2021.

he would one day marry classmate Laura Scheel. On December 30, 2016, he did just that.[27] We have all watched enough movies and read enough fairytales to have this assumption, that it seems that men and women cannot just be friends. One of them is bound to fall at some point.

My answer is yes, they can, but there are levels to this, yes. There are aspects of the friendship that need to be considered, such as the closeness of the friendship, and the intimacy of the friendship. I don't mean sex, because that would defeat the entire purpose of this conversation. I mean intimacy as a deep emotional connection, your comfort level with that person, how safe you feel with them, things like that. You can love someone deeply without being in love with that person. It's similar to familial love, but this family you created through bonds and experiences instead of blood.

Let me formally introduce you to Pedro. A best friend isn't even the right thing to call him because he is so much more than that. I used to call him brother, but people used to shade me constantly because they thought we should be together. The point is that is my boy; I swing first and ask questions later.

Pedro and I met in the ninth grade. It was early in the school year, and we sat next to each other in many of our classes, and our friendship just took off. The fact that people thought we were together, and to this day should be together, is a fault of our own making.

Sitting in gym class one hot Florida afternoon, we got into a conversation on dating. We came up with the bright idea of scamming the folks in our grade into thinking we were

---

27    Kelsey Borresen, "In Preschool, He Told His Class He Would Marry Her. And Then He Did," *HuffPost*, June 28, 2017.

together. In the morning, he would wait for me at the bus circle, and once the bell rang, he would walk me to class and leave with one of those lingering hugs. The bell would ring, signaling the end of class, and he would be there waiting to take me across the building. As the day came to an end, he would take my hand and wrap his arms around me as we walked back to the bus circle where the day began.

The cycle continued for a few weeks until people started taking us a little too seriously, the whispers in the halls were running rampant. We are a mess, I know, but who would have thought it would stick ten years later? We moved on, sort of, why everyone else couldn't!

We decided on the status of godparents in the ninth grade. (His current girlfriend, who is seemingly on track to be the misses, already knows I am to be the godmother.) He escorted me during my junior year pageant, and he was my date for homecoming. Very seemingly couple-y things for a pair of individuals who were not a couple, but that is just who we were and still are.

Throughout high school, past college, and even as post-grads, people have continued to ask why we haven't dated. The answer is, I don't know. I could try and hypothesize, but I guess it just wasn't in the cards for us.

I have this picture that he and I took at my twenty-fifth birthday dinner, and the caption is "Growing Up but not Apart." And it's a statement that has withstood the test of time. We went to college in different states and still live apart now, but whenever I see him, it's like I saw him yesterday. Nothing has changed.

I value his friendship in a profound way, because it constantly reminds me that I know how I deserve to be treated and that no man can waltz into my life thinking he can do whatever. Whomever the Lord decides to bless me with has to come correct because I can honestly say, "I had an amazing support system before you, and I will still have it after you if your act is not there." (You will read of a few slip-ups where I forgot this message, but I always remembered. . . eventually.)

Pedro and I hang out whenever I go home. It's the easiest date I go on constantly. All I have to do is call him, he tells me when he is not working, I pick a day and time, and he is there—no questions asked. Whenever we step out, I feel eyes on us, and it's like I can hear people thinking, "I wonder if they are together?" No, no we are not. Can we not go to dinner in peace?

While developing this chapter, it brought to the forefront of my mind the dynamics of my friendship with Pedro. Randomly at work, I decided to tell some coworkers about our friendship, explaining our "date nights," the development of our friendship through high school and college, after which they responded, "No wonder people think you guys are together." I laughed because this behavior is so normal for us. One night, we went to a party on South Beach that one of his Line Brother's was throwing. We stopped at the liquor store to get his friend a bottle as a gift, and we were not in the best neighborhood at the time, so Pedro was hovering behind me a bit, watching over me. I recall looking over my shoulder, and these guys were just staring at us and whispering. The whispering never ends. . . People have been whispering for fifteen years almost.

For a while, I didn't understand why this confused people. Eventually, I realized that not many people have such a deep connection with someone of the opposite sex without involving sex, and I think that's terrible. I know if I need a cheerleader, he's got me. If I need a protector, he's got me. If I just need someone to talk with to remind me who I am, he's got me. And I have all the emotional support on a platonic level. Here is where I must come clean. I'm not going to sit here and lie to you. At one point in my life I did "like" him. What's the point in being real if you're going to leave the good details out? I did have my little crush. Admittedly though, it was kind of on and off. Some months I felt like *yeah, I like him,* and sometimes I would feel as though, *nah, that's just my bestie.*

No one ever believed me though, because every time people would talk about him, I would just start smiling. I didn't realize being excited about talking about your friend automatically meant you had feelings, but that is their prerogative.

If you have a lingering question about whether anything has happened between us, the answer is yes. We made out once in the backseat of a car like some typical cliché teenage scenario. (Netflix, I have a new movie idea for you!)

It's funny because it happened that day, and we have never talked about it again—to let you guys in on the details.

Like a rational idiot, I decided to stop him once I found myself in his lap. You know, I am proud of teenage me and also hate her at the same time. When I pulled back, he looked at me curiously, and I just inhaled, you know, lack of oxygen and all. I told him that:

"We can't do this. You know if we do, it's not going to mean anything, and it might destroy us."

He sat there for a second milling over my words, and the resignation came to his eyes.

"You're right."

We sat there for about two minutes, just looking at each other not moving. It's almost like we were stuck in this trance of "what if?" There were too many questions and not enough solid answers. We shifted back to the front of the car, got lunch, and he took me home. Like I said, we have never talked about it since, but I do know the answer now to some of those "what ifs." One being that, honestly dating then going into college probably would have destroyed us. Pedro went through a deep college boy phase, as he was allowed to. That would not have been good for us.

Do I think he would have cheated on me? No, but I know me, and if he wanted to explore that life, would I have broken it off to let him? Thinking back on that afternoon, I think that was the first time I really acknowledged that there was something there. High school crushes can be fleeting, and I never took mine with him seriously. Also, back then, I never thought he would actually be interested in me. Guess I was wrong. What an interesting afternoon Pedro and I lived through.

When I was thinking about topics to add to this lovely book, he and I had a lot of conversations on multiple experiences and ideas that could be addressed. To start, he agrees dating in our generation is trash! Shout out to him for believing in me and reading my drafts and supporting what my book is now. Thank you for allowing me to share our story.

I have had my own theories and thoughts about why people would just assume we are a couple, and why things never happened between us. For me, I know how close we are, and I won't hesitate to take a nap on him, so most people just assume if you're that comfortable with someone, you are dating. In terms of being together, I was just like, *"The feelings are one-sided, that one time was a glitch, no biggie, happens all the time."* But then I got the bright idea to finally ask him his thoughts.

So I asked:

1. "Why do you think that some people assume we are a couple?"
2. "How do you feel about it?"
3. "Why do you think it never happened for us?"

His first response wasn't even an answer, he just enjoys being dramatic: "Spicy . . . I like it."

The actual responses go as follows:

1. "How close we are."
2. "I don't feel any ways toward it."
3. "Timing of where we were in our life."

Gotta love a straight answer. The thing I got out of those short answers was that I wasn't alone in my feelings. He felt the same, at least at some point. Things just didn't work, the timing was never right—ya know?

Chemistry is only part of the equation, the other is timing. Boy can timing really mess things up.

Remember earlier when we talked about how your friends say be patient, give it time, it'll happen, don't rush? Well, time is important, yes, but it can also be cruel. A lot of relationships that could have, should have, would have, have never been because of time. The timing was never right. The truth is, time has to be right for things to work.

Sometimes I wonder, *What if?* I question what could have been. I think it's natural to be curious, especially when what you have on a friendship level is so strong—imagine if those feelings were elevated. What if I had decided to go to school in Florida instead of going to Georgetown? What if I had stayed in Florida and decided to work instead of moving again for a job and so forth? The questions will be endless, but I already have my answer. As he likes to say, it is what it is.

Truthfully, I wouldn't give up what we have now. I believe we are where we are meant to be. I support him, and he supports me, and that is what matters. Our friendship is solid, and we love each other. I mean, I asked him if he would buy me food, and he sent me a whole large pizza, and I live alone. If that isn't love, I don't know what is. That's all we are all looking for, right? A little love?

I believe men and women can just be friends—you just have to be equally prepared to go on the roller coaster it entails. I promise you if you stick it out with the right person, it can be a lot of fun. They will be there to help you through the first dates you have been stood up for, the heartbreaks, and the days you don't feel like it's ever going to work. They remind you to love yourself just as much as, if not more than, they love you.

The best analogy I could give is, for anyone who has watched *Criminal Minds*, that Morgan and Penelope's friendship is what we have. Based off of their dynamic, I truly believe that every girl, woman, whomever you are, deserves to be treated the way Morgan treats Penelope. That is Morgan's baby girl, and that's what I am lucky enough to have. I do believe every girl deserves a guy like that in their life, regardless of who or where they are, it's different and effortless, you don't have those relationship expectations, and you can just be yourself.

I have a coworker who lives with her guy friend who she has known since college. Ashley is a few years older than I am, and in comparison to Pedro and me, Ashley and her roommate have been friends just as long. She will straight up tell you never once in her life has she seen him as more than a friend, as she boldly told me that is not someone that she wants in her bed. Ashley's roommate enjoys watching bad TV in bed, making cookies, and binging on the couch as a friend. His style is nothing close to going out, dressed to the nines, and planning staycations. They argue about paper towels. The difference is clear, and this is what I like to call "domestically platonic."

This is why blanket statements like claiming men and women are not able to just be friends is problematic. The answer to the question, to me, is still yes. But after further analysis, the more accurate answer is, it depends on who you ask.

In conclusion, I believe you can be friends with a guy and never see them any other way. Or you can meet a guy and feel something immediately. You can also meet a guy, be friends with him, and either gradually or unexpectedly fall for him. Finally, you can be friends, gradually fall for them, and still have that timing never, ever work out for you because you are just destined to be a godmother.

The point is, go out there and be open-minded. Relationships take so many forms, so do not cut yourself off because of misguided assumptions. Do I love my best friend? Yes. Am I in love with my best friend? No. Could I fall in love with him? Sure. Now go watch *Criminal Minds* Season four, Episode one.

# SHOULDA, WOULDA, COULDA

———

*I Shoulda: I should have said something sooner.*
*I Woulda: What would we have been?*
*I Coulda: We could have been amazing.*

Dating is truly just the luck of the draw sometimes. You could pluck a goldfish one time, and the next time reel in a king salmon. The question is, how does one enter the river? Simple, it's asking someone out. A 2017 Match.com survey of 5,509 single men and women showed that 95 percent of men were in favor of a woman asking for their number — but only 13 percent of women were game to do it.[28]

I believe, for the most part, women still want men to make that first move. It is such a peculiar balance. I've had guy friends tell me that they're sometimes too nervous to approach a woman they're interested in. For them, the

———

28 Brittany Wong, "Women on Twitter Are Sharing What Happens When They Ask Crushes out on a Date," *HuffPost*, October 27, 2017.

woman making the first move would be ideal, even sexy. A woman going after what *she* wants, that *is* sexy.

Me personally, I hate making the first move. I start tripping over my words, my anxiety spikes, it is not a good look for a first impression at all. It's why I have issues with Bumble. I think it's just part of this ever-confusing social construct of what dating is "supposed" to look like, coupled with that good ole fashioned fear of rejection.

If you google "Should women ask men out?" you get a lot of conflicting material. For example, Evan Marc Katz, a dating coach and author, wrote a blog post titled "Should Women Ask Men out on First Dates?" and his answer was, "No. No, they should not. Women asking men on first dates can be taken as aggressive, desperate, and masculine. At the very least, it can signify a loss of power. So, I wouldn't recommend that you ever utter the words, 'Would you like to go out with me?' to any man."[29]

However on the flip side, you have Starre Vartan, and while she is not immersed in dating professionally like Evan, she wrote a piece in *Treehugger that I found interesting, titled: "Why Women Should Ask Men out on More Dates." She breaks her answer down into multiple points:*

1. "Women never get to choose: When women are socially sanctioned to wait for a guy to ask them out, it's dis-empowering. It leaves the women's perceptions and desires out of the equation; they can only choose from among the men who have already chosen them.

2. Men don't hate it (Sorry Evan, she does have a point): Men are open to being asked out. It's flattering. They may say

---

29  Evan Marc Katz, "Should Women Ask Men Out on First Dates?," *Dating Coach - Evan Marc Katz | Understand Men. Find Love*, January 18, 2021.

yes, or they may say no, but all the guys said they would never say no to a date simply because a woman initiated it.

3. It's a lot of pressure on men: Asking someone out means you have to put your ego on the line. That makes some people more nervous than others. Not all men will react the same way to that anxiety; it's harder on some then others, but being expected to always do the asking is an unfair pressure on guys. (Type A guys versus busy guys versus shy guys, you know there are so many . . .)

4. Women don't get to practice rejection: Asking out a person who you don't know all that well carries a significant chance of rejection. Practicing this kind of small failure is good for anyone; it gets you more used to dealing with it in other areas of life. (other areas include negotiating higher pay. Get those coins, sis!)

   a. It can lead to harassment: When only one gender is "supposed" to do the, it sometimes leads to misunderstandings, or worse. When men are taught to "go after the woman they want," it can lead to guys not taking "no thanks" for an answer.

5. It leads to fewer dates overall: If only one side is doing the asking that's only half of the dating potential involved. Dating is a numbers game, so it benefits anyone who's looking for company to up those numbers in their favor."[30]

Every argument has two different and distinct sides. Where are you going to stand? How about both? If you are interested, you can dive deeper into Evan's article, but here are the CliffsNotes. It depends on the guy. While it may seem like men are meant to be the aggressor, not all men are. Some

---

30  Starre Vartan, "Why More Women Should Ask Men Out on Dates," *Tree-hugger*, accessed October 6, 2020.

are shy and fear rejection as well. In these cases, it's going to be up to the woman to pick up that torch and make a run. It doesn't matter what society thinks, what matters is between you and that person.

Picture this: You're at a lounge with some friends, and you see an attractive young man looking at your table. He seems to have been giving you eyes all night, but you aren't sure.

*Is he looking at me?*

*Is he looking at someone I am with?*

*Should I just take the plunge and get up?*

*Could I be embarrassing myself?*

*Would I survive this rejection?*

*Is he a Type A personality where he has to make the move?*

*Is he quiet?*

I think inner strength plays a big role in this sort of situation, or as some call it, confidence. The point being, some of us are definitely more confident than others. People who can take charge and go after what they want, I applaud you. However, I think a lot of people are like myself: not reserved, but too scared to take charge without a serious pep talk.

The pep talks I have to give myself to do things are in a constant loop. Like so many other people, I'm scared of rejection, so unless approached, your girl is keeping her mouth shut! Now, I have broken this vow of silence twice in my life; one ended in disaster, the other worked out pretty nicely. My hope is, that by the end of this chapter, despite my personal battle, you find the courage to be open and realize that while rejection does hurt, the worst they can say is no. Plus, at least you would finally have an answer, so you aren't pining for someone with no direction in sight.

First things first, I am totally an advocate for women going after what they want. I know we have been taught our whole lives that if a guy wants you, he will let you know, and this theory is true sometimes, as Evan taught us earlier. However, I have learned, in my limited practice, this isn't always the case, as Starre pointed.

Full disclosure, while I'm no longer with the man I'm about to speak about, I felt this story was too important not to mention. After second guessing myself for months, I finally decided to take the plunge, and it worked.

Ever since I was in college, I worked part-time in a bakery. When I started working full-time after graduation, I decided to keep it as my side hustle to save up some money. It's crazy how distinctly I remember the first time I saw this man. I had just turned twenty-three and was working that weekend in March. I remember having to be there at 7 a.m. instead of 8 a.m. those days because we were so busy. Decked out in my standard black t-shirt and workout-leggings. It was about 60 degrees that day because DC decided it wanted to be spring that day.

On Saturdays, we receive our ingredient delivery. It's usually a guy just catering in five hundred pounds worth of butter, sugar, milk, and flour. It was such a regular occurrence that I didn't really pay it any mind. Sometimes we saw the delivery guy, and other times we didn't, it depended on the time of the delivery, but this morning my eyes were blessed.

Around 9 a.m., in walks this 6'3" combination of caramel and mocha gorgeous smiling man. I am so embarrassed to admit that after staring at him for a moment I ran. Not out of the store, thankfully, but I ran right into the office, looking for someone to bring me back down to Earth. I told you guys I am bad at this, so consider my point proven. I found the assistant manager and half whispered:

"There is a fine man in our store."

As any curious woman would, she turned and looked at me asking "Where?" I pointed her to the camera, and we both shamelessly appraised this man from afar. After about five minutes, I re-centered myself and went back to work, stealing glances here and there. When he left, he smiled at me, and what a smile it was. He made my whole day and didn't even know. That was what we did from March until October. For six, almost seven, months, he would come in every Saturday, and we would smile at each other. Eventually, we spiced things up by adding *Hello* to the mix, though it was a very mild spice. Eventually, I worked my way to medium spice and gave him a box of cupcakes. Since I couldn't get a single word out of my mouth that meant something, I figured I could give him little reminders of my existence.

By this point, all the friends I worked with knew I had a crush on him. It was getting ridiculous. One day it was pouring, giving my mind time to process things, and it hit me, in all this time (it was now October) I didn't even know his name. It was so cold and gloomy out, I was moving around, trying to stay warm, and contemplating whether or not breakfast was going to be a cupcake, when my future bae arrived with our delivery. . . but I got to see my future bae. While he was outside unloading ingredients, I mentioned to my friend that I didn't even know his name. She then bet me that I wouldn't ask him name.

Now most days she would have been right. However, today I was feeling bold. I looked her right in her eye, picked up my umbrella, and marched outside to ask him. As I exited the store, I started thinking to myself, *Girl, what is wrong with you, it's raining out here, you could've waited 'til he came inside. You know he is going to think something is wrong with you, right?*

1. I was too far gone from the front door at this point.
2. I knew I couldn't have done it in front of them.

So, I continued to the truck, and called out to him.

"Hey," I said. I could hear the tremble in his voice.

He turned around and looked at me in surprise.

"I have a question." I was surprised by my authority, considering the hello.

He nodded his head for me to continue.

"What's your name?"

He looks at me for a second, taken aback.

"Derrick," he replied.

"Hi, Derrick. I'm Nicole." That was the end of that.

Now, the mature thing to do would have been to ask him how his morning was, right? To ensure that the conversation didn't end in awkward silence. Nope, my social skills came to a grinding halt. I turned on my heels and booked it inside. Being suave is not something I'm good at. If anyone thinks I'm kidding, my friends recorded the whole exchange. I still have the video, so I can always watch myself act like a fool.

I appreciate how well he took that interaction, because internally I was mess. As he was bringing the sacks of flour in a few minutes later, he paused in front of the counter where I was working. I looked up at him. He chuckled at me and said,

"You know, my name is on my shirt," and then proceeded to point at the upper left corner of his polo. It's a good thing I have so much melanin, otherwise, I would have been so red with embarrassment. As he closed the box in front of me, I looked up at him.

"Good to know."

In an attempt to redeem myself, I threw him a million-dollar smile with a red velvet as he left for the morning.

A few weeks pass, we were still smiling, and we had established names, which is a step in the right direction. One Saturday, I got another idea! I realized that all of this could have been done in one weekend, but bear with me. He is usually in the store for thirty minutes anyway.

I was going to leave him a note, via cupcakes. I think *What the hell, I only see him once a week anyway.* By now, this had become our thing. While I packed him a box, I wrote a note inside... "I hope you have a good day," and I drew a smiley face, you know, 'cause we smile a lot. The risk factor, while disastrous, was minimal. If he wasn't into it, then I'd have a whole week to pretend like it didn't happen and find a new job. I sealed the box and my fate with Derrick. When he was done, I handed him the box and off he went until next Saturday.

Shockingly, I wasn't a mess all week wondering what Saturday would bring, but when I saw that truck pull up, I was a total ball of nerves. He walked in and smiled at me and proceeded to take things to the back. I leaned back into the view of the hallway of where he walked wondering, *Well, he smiled, so that's a good sign, but is he going to address the note?* He started walking back to the front of the store as I was in the walkway. Instead of continuing through, he stopped, turned to me while he was leaning forward on the dolly and says,

"Thank you for the note, but I was kind of hoping I would find your number."

I had saucer eyes. Without a response from me, he continued through the front door to grab more things. I stood there stunned for like twenty seconds, and then my legs caught up to my brain. Much like the first day I ever saw him, I hightailed my ass right back to the office (here I go running...

again) in dire need of a pen, marker, Sharpie, or any other type of writing utensil. Ironically enough, Mel was in the office again, just as she was in March when I first saw him.

The store always seems to eat writing instruments at the most inopportune times. Reminiscent of our previous exchanges, this one with a different promise, I handed him his box with an extra detail inside. He bid me goodbye with a smile. He finally had my number! *insert high pitched squeal* I was ready to break out into a one-person flash mob in front of the store.

He reached out Sunday, responding to my message in the box.

"Now that I can talk to you, yes, it is better." Derrick is a charmer, that one. We played twenty questions for days, getting to know one another past fleeting weekly glances. I had this crazy smile on my face for a week. On the first day, we talked about any and everything. Work, hobbies, his love for cooking. Ladies, I 10/10 recommend finding a man who cooks—it is a game changer. That crab mac and cheese he made one night was the key to my heart. As our conversation started winding down, he invited me to watch the Cowboys with him that day. I quickly accepted without really thinking the logistics through.

He lived about an hour away from me, and as I thought about it, I realized it would take me an hour to get home and then an hour to his place, so me going home was useless. However, I was not about to roll up to his home dressed the way I was. That Sunday, by the end of my shift, I had donned a black shirt with glove powder, buttercream frosting, and confectioners' sugar, paired with black leggings sprinkled in confectioners' sugar. Even though this was the only state he had seen me in, I had to step my game up.

When my shift was over, I shamelessly went shopping and bought a whole new outfit and booties. It was the epitome of trying without looking like I was trying too hard, and any women who have been on a first date know exactly what I am talking about. There is a fine distinction in putting in effort, while making that effort look effortless. As though you do this all the time even though you know you spend most of your life in leggings. Extra detail: I did go to his house in an oversized sweater and leggings—sue me. It was fall; a classic October look for me.

As a football fan, I was excited, and the company was just the sugar on top. He temporarily converted me to being a Cowboys fan, made me dinner, and we had a great night. True to his gentleman ways, he drove an hour to take me home and left with a warm kiss to my temple.

Sundays became the day we would hang out and watch football. I even took possession of his Cowboys shirt. For our first date, he took me out for sushi, where we learned we both had a love for Marvel. Granted, things didn't work out for us, and this chapter is not about those nitty gritty details, but I wanted to show what swallowing your fear can bless you with. Dating, relationships, love, none of that comes with a guarantee of success, but you do miss all the shots you don't take.

It was a blessing even if it didn't last because I really liked this man. One night after one of our dates, we were in his movie room watching some action movie. I was invested in the movie, but Derrick was too invested in me to know what was going on the screen. Now that I think about it, I think he picked a movie he had already seen just for that reason. He spent an hour and forty-five minutes drawing patterns on the right side of my body. I was laying my head in his lap, bought into everything Tom Cruise was saying on the screen.

I did notice what he was doing but he didn't have to know that. At least not yet.

The movie ended, and I rotated so I was now flat on my back and looking up at him. He smiled at me and started playing with my hand. Physical touch is one of my love languages, so I was soaking up the affection like a sponge. I brought myself into a seating position in his lap, we were now nose to nose, and I tilted my head ever so slightly and kissed him. We stayed in that position for a while. My favorite part is the words out of his mouth after this. The man had a slick mouth. He kissed my neck and proceeded to whisper in my ear. . .

"Do you want to make a baby?"

*Whatttttt. . .*

Now, I am a one-liner comeback queen, so while shocked, I was not going to let him get me.

"How about you ask me that again in a few years. Will practice do for now?"

He threw his head back laughing while I just looked at him. Then he got this glint in his eye, which only meant trouble. He picked me up and threw me over his shoulder, casually striding out of the room while I begged him to put me down.

*We all know I didn't want to, but pretenses are important.*

I called Kat, my best friend, immediately the next morning. Admittedly, I did entertain what an actual future with him would look like a few times. At the time, I was seriously considering going back to school. Kat does not miss a beat if she is invested in a subject. She said. . .

"Even if you do go to grad school in New York, you could always come down on weekends. Plus, there is nothing wrong being pregnant towards the end."

*I know this bitch did not say pregnant. Why are we all now cosigning this joke?*

My friends are wild. I don't regret dating him the same way I have regretted some exes. I asked him one night why he didn't ask me out sooner. He told me that he had developed a liking for me for a while but held back.

"I held back, I didn't want to come off too strong and then you feel uncomfortable because I'm there every week."

A man that cares about your feelings is such a rarity in my experience. Granted I could talk about the messed-up way he and I stopped talking but we not going to drag him. . . not yet. Stay tuned.

Ladies sometimes we got to make the first move, put on our big girl panties, and do what needs to get done. I know I am a hypocrite, because most times I am not this girl, but I am working on it. Dating is just so rough in general, and it's so much easier to hide. This would also be a good time for all of us to admit that we are all a little scared. Some of us are just better at hiding it than others. If you are just that solid and do not get scared, please teach me your ways.

You may not always get what you want, it's a risk to ask a man out. It's a risk when he asks you out, so why not attempt to level the playing field? It could work out, it could not, it could for a little bit and then who knows? Relationships don't come with a lifetime guarantee, and there definitely isn't a warranty on them, but what if he is the one?

*"You don't get it, I don't get it, Let's just go with it."*
- *Unknown*

# IT JUST HAPPENED

---

*"She said. . . .*
*"He was never mine but losing him broke my heart*
*I felt that"*[31]

*DJ, PLEASE PLAY DAMAGE BY H.E.R.*

Depending on the movies you watch, falling in love can be such a beautiful experience, it can be unexpected, or it can flip your life upside down in a good way. However, movies never really tell you about the dark side of falling or the fact that you can fall for the wrong person. Falling in love with the wrong person or at the wrong time can shatter you. He was never meant to be mine from the start, and I always knew that. I played myself into the false reality that kept telling me that it was ok. Our whole relationship was on a countdown; we just didn't know when, why, or how it would end. While I wish three years ago, I had made a different decision, if to do nothing but save myself from the tears that unexpectedly

---

31  Bella Quint (@bellaquintt), " "She said…He was never mine but losing him broke my heart" I felt that," Twitter, December 1, 2020, 3:06 a.m.

appear when I think about him too much, I know in my heart I do not actually regret it. I think in its own twisted way, I needed this.

I needed to know what it was like to love someone and lose them. I needed to know what it was like to put someone first and subsequently be a priority. I needed to know what it was like to give it my all and still find myself alone. I needed the truth that only experience could bring. It takes work to keep that ideal image of love. It takes two people centered on the same goal for any relationship to succeed. No one person can carry a relationship, no matter how much I wanted to fool myself. I needed to accept that some people do change and that it didn't have a single thing to do with me. I needed to learn that it was ok to love myself more and to recognize that his love wasn't enough. This didn't make me a bad person.

Let me formally introduce you to Damien and tell you about the journey to my love lesson.

Damien is such an anomaly in my life. I can't really tell you where he came from. One day he was just there and never left. Much like his appearance in my life, the growth of our friendship was just as random. We went from maybe talking three to four times in a year for the first few years of our friendship to practically speaking every day about any and everything up until now.

Damien is a cutie, and just because we aren't together anymore doesn't mean I am going to discount his looks. He wasn't *Damn, Daniel* fine, he was one of those people whose looks grew on you. He was 6'3" (clearly I have a thing for tall men), with a caramel complexion, bright, mischievous eyes, and a contagious smile. He loved to randomly sing and dance, and like many of us he would put on concerts in his car. What attracted me to him was his personality. He had such a dry sense of humor, but he was always so willing to be a listening ear. He was so supportive of me in everything and was like my daily dose of positive reinforcement. When I sit back and think about it, he reminds me a lot of Pedro, which is maybe why I was drawn to him.

When I moved to DC, Damien and I really became besties. He would call or text me at least twice a week to check up on me. As the months went on, so did the frequency of his calls. He would ask me questions about my non-existent love life. I would tell him about the date attempts, where one would ask but never follow through. He always told me to keep my head up. I was too pretty to not find someone who would appreciate me. *Hmmm. . . If only I knew then what I know now.*

He made me a video of him singing for my birthday. For like three years straight, he won the game of first text on my birthday. It just felt nice to have someone so invested in my well-being. Like I mentioned, one of the things I loved about him was his personality. Included in the personality was how he was the personification of relationship goals.

If you were wondering why I didn't date him early, it was because. . . *ding, ding,* he had a girlfriend. I swear all the good ones are taken. They were everything I wanted in a relationship, and to an extent that is still true. They were low key, but when they did bless our timeline with a photo, you could see the love between them. They used to work alternating shifts a few months out of the year, so he made Thursdays their date nights and would plan these sweet dates for her. It was all very heart warming and straight out of some Hallmark film.

Around the time of his birthday, Damien started acting a little weird. I could not quite put my finger on it. He was being a little bit flirtier and forward than normal. In the back of my head, I was so confused because I could have sworn, he and his girl were still together. I would later come to learn that was not the case. At the time, though, I didn't know that, so when his comments went a little left, I proceeded with caution. I am guilty of indulging him one night.

I was truly gobsmacked by the time he was done. Who knew. . .? The conversation ended, and we never addressed it again, so things went back to normal. A few weeks later, I celebrated my birthday. Midnight on the dot his message came through.

He and I went to dinner, in celebration of my birthday, a few days later. That's when he dropped the bombshell that he and his girl had split, and it had been a few months. I was heartbroken for him. He wasn't much of a talker, so the fact that we spent so much time going over what happened was astonishing. I like to think he felt safe enough to share his thoughts with me. We finished dinner, he drove me home, I left him with a hug goodbye, and he drove off.

We agreed to hang out the next day after he finished running some errands. We were aiming to meet at 6 p.m., but he was still out helping a friend. To kill some time, I took myself to dinner, sat in a booth, and watched the basketball game that was on. One chicken quesadilla and Celtics win later, I left and headed back to my car. I called him to see where he was. Damien and I were mid-conversation when I looked up to see my ex walk past. (I call him my ex because that is the easiest way to explain what he was in my life even though we were never "actually" together). I think I was answering a question, and I just stopped mid-sentence. He was calling my name to get my attention, and for like ten seconds, my brain didn't even register his voice.

Eventually his voice filtered through the fog, and I told him what I witnessed. In my head, I have envisioned at least three scenarios where I get out of this car and approach my ex. (Things did not end well between us. Maybe I'll talk about him in the sequel.) To avoid invoking any of the petty behavior that is now on loop in my brain, Damien all but demanded I come over right now. In hindsight, he probably did save me from doing something stupid, I just didn't realize I was setting myself up for something even more serious, giving my heart up to someone.

Side bar: This was all a setup, I swear, because what are the odds. It was getting so late that I was about to head home and see Damien the next day instead.

I made the drive over to his place; I never drive, so it was a nice change of pace. I pulled into his driveway and instead of going inside, we sat in the car and watched the night sky along with the twinkling stars. We talked about how he was doing, work, food, music. I started playing the *Hamilton* soundtrack for some reason. "Cabinet Battle #1" is still a banger. We talked and talked for hours; we were in this little bubble, as if nothing else existed outside of this car but us.

I wish I could explain the progression of the next sequence of events, but honestly, I don't know. All I know is one minute we are talking and the next I found myself wrapped in his arms, secure in his lap with absolutely no intentions of moving. He looked at me with an intrigue in his eyes and then leaned up and kissed me. I remember how soft his lips were, how I just melted in his arms, and how everything in my mind went blank. I remember how smooth his hands were, and with just a touch, a callous reminded me that he worked with his hands. At one point we had exited the car to enjoy the cool of the night air. I was leaning back on the trunk trapped between his arm, attempting to fake fight my way out. In true Damien fashion, he laughed at me and proceeded to pick me up and place me on the trunk. He gave me a peck and then pulled back, looking at me so intently my heart started to stammer. He leaned back in, kissing me again with this passion that I felt from head to toe. I could have stayed their all night without a care in the world. This went on for like two hours.

*Who would have thought, because I certainly did not!*

Two make out sessions and a conversation later, I reluctantly removed myself from his arms. He opened my door and placed me back in the car. With a kiss to the forehead, he bid me "good morning." Confused by his statement I looked at the dash and almost screamed. The clock blinked back at me 4 a.m. We had been in and out of this car in his driveway for almost six hours.

"Think you got moves, huh?"

"Well, I've kept you here for six hours. . . so, I would hope."

I did the most adult thing I could do, stuck my tongue out at him, and drove home.

I wasn't home for more than two minutes before I was screaming over text to my best friend about what had just happened. I was so confused; I did not know what to think or feel. Damien and I are supposed to just be friends. None of his flirty comments were supposed to mean anything. They were supposed to just be words. However, based on the last few hours of my life, there might have been some actual substance to those conversations, which both terrified and intrigued me.

Intrigue won over fear, and here we are two years later. It was the intrigue that got me where I am now. He evoked something in me that night, I did not know what it was, but I was curious to find out. I remember texting him that morning, since, you know, the sun was about to rise in an hour, asking him:

"What now?"

"Now, you learn about a side of me that you only ever heard about but now get to experience."

Experience I did.

Our relationship, which technically was a situationship—but for the purpose of keeping to the theme we shall call a relationship—was not a physical one. . . in the beginning, well, for almost a year. It was all rooted in the emotional connection we had with each other. Not that we did not fool around, but there was no rush to cross that bridge.

We talked every day, all day, for months. He would check on me every morning and FaceTime me during the day. We used to fall asleep on the phone entirely too many times, more than I can count. If he couldn't reach me, he would usually just text me, but once he left me this voicemail, and it was so sweet.

"Good morning, just calling to check on you. I haven't heard your cute voice in a while. But you're probably searching for your headphones, so I'm going to leave you a voicemail, I don't care, later. I love—and here you go, calling me now."

He was right about the headphones by the way. For the first time in a while, I felt special and important. I got to know him in a way that was so much more intimate. We talked about his future and my future. Every time we were together, I was blissfully happy. Every text, phone call, and hug came with a plastered smile and a desire to fight myself for it every time. I knew we were not together and would never actually be together. Why, may you ask? Because I knew there was a solid 85 percent chance he would get back with his ex. I was playing myself into this false security. Damien was my escape, and I was his. An escape from the world that did not quite understand us, to a place where we understood each other. An escape into a place where we knew that we were safe with each other and cared for by one another.

We used to have real fights like we were a couple, and it would boggle my mind because it would be so easy to say, "fuck this," and walk away, but while the framework wasn't real, the emotions unfortunately were.

The first time we were intimate, it solidified. . .

- How I had unintentionally fallen in love with this man (yikes).
- How I was right that having an emotional connection makes everything better.

That whole first year and most of the second, I got a taste of the type of relationship I had wanted. We had similar interests but also had many differences. I learned new things every day. I would help him study for his classes over Face-Time. He helped me shop for shoes. We were each other's escape until reality came back.

The whole relationship was beautiful and messy and loving and fucked up and whatever other adjective you can think of, but I got what it meant to be blinded. I just wanted someone to understand me, be there for me through the good and bad, and he was that and more for so long that when it all changed, it shattered my heart even though I knew it was bound to happen.

He started being distant, would go days without talking to me, which was unheard of. We would fight about his sudden lack of communication. No matter how many times he promised to try, it never quite stuck. I just got tired. A relationship can't sustain itself if it feels like only one person is fighting for it. Time passed, the days of silence just keep getting longer and longer. I guess the clock finally timed out.

I sit and look at my phone at messages that have been left on read. Questions completely left unanswered as though my existence is non-existent. It's like I don't matter, and the truth is, maybe I don't. Maybe I have lost my "purpose" in his life now that things are different and he has a new mission. Maybe it is just easier to pretend that I am not here. Out of sight, out of mind.

But I am here. I do exist, and I do matter. As much as I would give it all back, give every kiss, hug, and "I love you" back just to have my friend back, I don't think I ever will, and that is ok. Loving Damien taught me a lot of things: it taught me so much good and unfortunately showed me a lot of reality as well. It reinforced my deep-rooted desire for intimacy. The type of intimacy where just knowing he was around made me feel safe. A simple hug washed away all the troubles in my mind. There are times that I have texted him just requesting a hug and he would show up just to give me that hug. Early on, when I asked about his take on PDA, he responded. . .

"I am the type of guy who will walk behind you in the grocery store with my arms wrapped around your middle just to feel you near me."

Did I have a personal swoon moment? Yes. Am I ashamed? Not in the slightest.

My relationship with Damien also taught me the importance of relationships. It brought to light that actions definitely speak so much louder than words. He revealed that if I have to repeat the same thing fifteen million times, it's not me, it's him. There is no "fixing" someone; if they wanted to do it, they would. I know what Damien was like when he wanted me, and I had to deal with the fact that it wasn't the same anymore. Life is not always going to be about the good days; it is about how you power through the bad ones and give yourself grace so that you can truly enjoy those amazing days we are blessed with.

We have spoken a few times since and decided to be adults and settle on the title of friends. He and his girl never did get back together. Every now and then you can feel that crackle in the air of something being there. I don't know if it will go away. Even now I think we might have to disown him from the island permanently, but we will see, and I will keep you guys posted!

I've always wanted him to be happy the same way I want to be happy. Love is interesting because of the way it can transform. Do I love him? I would be a liar if I say I don't, but love isn't enough.

"My last relationship taught me A LOT. It taught me not to ignore signs & my gut feeling. I learned how to love myself & not to put anyone above my happiness & my dreams. Now I know my worth, know what I want, & I won't settle for less again. No regrets, I needed to learn those lessons."[32]

*Play:* Know Your Worth *by Khalid & Disclosure*

---

32  Sza fans (@itssza), "My last relationship taught me A LOT. It taught me not to ignore signs & my gut feeling. I learned how to love myself & not to put anyone above my happiness & my dreams. Now I know my worth, know what I want, & I won't settle for less again. No regrets, I needed to learn those lessons.", Twitter, February 2, 2018, 2:36 p.m.

# AIN'T NO WRATH LIKE. . .

---

I know, I did not deep dive into the nitty-gritty of my breakup with Damien, and I didn't for a reason. I wanted to address it separately. In the last chapter, I laid it out as though I accepted my life lessons. Sure, things hurt, but I am a big girl and I can handle my emotions. Honestly, that would be the biggest lie ever. I was mad, I was angry, I debated hundreds of ways to cuss him out from here to next Sunday. I just never followed through. I figured keeping the peace was the best thing I could do. Even though I was tired of him treating me like I was some basic girl he had just met in a grocery store. He probably will read this and know I am talking about him.

Anyone who knows me knows that I am a gym rat. Bash Boxing was and still is one of the best things that happened to me. With the emotional roller coaster I was on dealing with Damien toward the end, I might have actually fought him in the streets (well at least tried to) if it hadn't been for my boxing studio. Shout out to them for helping me not give him a black eye. Damien had such potential, but he drove me crazy.

I think communication skills are one of the sexiest things a man can have. You could eventually lose those biceps I love so much, but if we can still talk to one another, I think we are good. I do not need the typical brooding type of guy. Ben Affleck is already playing Batman; I do not need you trying to secure the brooding role.

Unfortunately, Damien was one of those people. I expressed this earlier as well. If you do not want to spill your guts to me, that is completely fine, but don't shut me out completely. A little heads up is all I was requesting.

I understand that people process emotions in different ways. However, like I said before when you are involved with someone, you need to be cognizant of your behaviors and patterns, and subsequently how they affect other people. People can very easily fall into this pattern of "me, me, me," forgetting there are others involved who care about you and just want to make sure you are ok. When it came to him, I learned when to just let him have his time. Other times I pushed, and you know what? He did not spontaneously combust. He may have momentarily not liked it, but eventually, he appreciated the push.

I had hoped because I was open to being flexible to his needs, he would do the same. Relationships are about give and take. The answer to that would be he started but diverted off course somewhere else.

We saw each other sporadically throughout the year. Distance and hectic schedules are truly a pain. The holiday season was rapidly descending upon us, and we were trying to fit in time to see each other. His job had this huge project that they were closing out in the beginning of the new year, but they had a small reprieve right after Christmas. He called me a few days leading up to Thanksgiving, asking me if I would be back by then. Due to my job, I had to be back the day after Christmas, but for him I was willing to make the exception and come back early regardless. December 29 was the date, and I was so excited I was finally getting to see my baby.

I scoured my apartment top to bottom, sheets washed, towels softened, carpet vacuumed, grocery list made for when I returned from Christmas with my own family. I left to enjoy Christmas with my family. He and I had spoken the night before, but we didn't talk the following day, which, given his schedule, wasn't weird, so I didn't think much of it at the time.

My phone is usually dry, but now I was just seeing tumbleweeds roll by. Even though I am used to a certain level of silence from him, I began getting a little concerned, but it was nothing to call the FBI about. A few more days go by, and now all alarm bells are firing off. I kid you not, I scrolled back through our last conversation to make sure nothing crazy was said. I have this bad habit of thinking that it is something I have done and I need to fix it, when in actuality, I have not done anything and there is nothing for me to fix.

Christmas goes by, nothing—and you guys, this was the day he and I almost stopped being friends, let alone whatever the fuck you would label us at the time. I have to explain what caused me to almost sever ties on the spot.

On Christmas Eve, I spent the day baking some cakes for my mom. I love to bake, and when I do, I tend to capture the journey on my Snapchat story. After posting the story, I started scrolling through my friends list, watching their stories, when I came across his profile. Part of me wanted to resist, and the other part of me could not have clicked this circle fast enough. I watched it like a masochist, and even writing this is giving me horrendous flashbacks.

As the story plays, my left eyebrow starts to rise, I start to recognize the streets he was driving on. My thoughts started to head to violence. . .

*You are not where you told me you would be a few weeks ago, you are in the same state as me, as a matter of fact, you are currently about fifteen minutes away from my house.*

The words left my mouth before my brain could filter anything; I stood there dumbfounded.

*What the actual fuck, Damien.*

You know what they say—when a woman is screaming and yelling, you still have a chance to fix things. However, if she is silent and calm, you're screwed. I quietly picked up my phone. I walked outside and called my best friend and started ranting. (He was lucky because I almost got in my car and started driving.) My brain could not comprehend how on Earth we could be in the same state, let alone the same city, and he wouldn't even say anything. The petty side of me wanted nothing more than to roll up on him and start demanding answers. The rational side of Nikki won out. My butt stayed planted at home, I enjoyed my holiday, and I went back to work. I say Nikki because I was still pissed, and had I seen him in the streets, the jump-off would have occurred. We were each spared what could have easily been a brawl.

When I got back, I went to Bash, fought him in a safe space, and tried to pretend as though nothing was wrong. If he could keep pushing with his life, then so could I.

*Week 1-* It's fine.

*Week 2 -* This is what we are doing.

*Week 3-* Wowwwww

*Week 4-* I sent him a text about how him being quiet is unfair and how I don't appreciate his complete disregard of my feelings.

*Week 5* - He really left me on read.

*Week 6* - I give up.

At this point, we are in the month of February, and a tragedy has hit us all. We had just found out that Kobe Bryant had died, and truthfully, I was a mess. Something in me just couldn't handle the emotions I was feeling, and I reverted back to old habits. Whether I did it consciously or unconsciously, I called Damien. I do not recall exactly what I said in the voicemail because he didn't answer the phone. I just remember being so torn up inside and crying. My brain has the tendency to go completely left when I read tragic stories. All I could think was that if something ever happened, I didn't want him to think I hated him or something.

Of course, I fell asleep and my phone died, so I missed his call later that night. The next morning, we talked, and it was the most anticlimactic conversation I ever had. Which honestly was probably a good thing, no need to start breaking dishes in the kitchen at work. I did find out his original travel plans fell through, and that is why he decided to disappear from the world or keep to himself (the answer depends on which one of us you ask). To each their own, and like I said previously, everyone processes things differently. I won't hold that against him, this was something he was really looking forward to.

What upset me was his response to one of my questions. In his six weeks of silence, I reached out trying to clear the air, and just to be honest with the fact that him bouncing just didn't sit right with me, regardless of how we felt about each other, because at the very least we were friends. His response was:

"If I was just going to be done then fine."

I remember standing in that kitchen dumbfounded, thinking:

*So our friendship didn't matter to you at all, you weren't even going to attempt to fix this misunderstanding, just nothing.*

I remember feeling so defeated. Is it me, do I just care too much about people? After everything we have been through, this was the best you could come up with. I almost preferred the silence to this.

We were in a rocky place for a while. Much like the cycle of our relationship, we were like magnets, and the pull never faded. Slowly, things started to normalize again, but I was still a little wary of him. One Saturday, we had a tell-all therapy session, one of three we had probably had by this point. For me, I felt like maybe we were finally getting somewhere, and that he understood my point of view. I am not some crazy person who is permanently stuck in her feelings. I expressed to him,

"Your silence is not what bothers me, it's your lack of presence that I have issues with. You want to be part of my life, but I am always the one putting in the effort to keep us afloat."

"I want to do better and be more present. I know I have not been doing the best job, but I am here for you."

It's those damn eyes that get me every time. I swallowed my snarky ass comment. Pretended to be an adult, built a bridge, and got over it.

A few weeks later, he surprised me with a plane ticket. When he asked if I wanted to do something spontaneous, I 100 percent thought he was joking. He proved me wrong. We spent the weekend together, and it's a weekend I hold very dear to my heart.

You may now be wondering why, if things seem settled, I am even talking about this. Well, it's because I seem to have the worst luck ever.

When we first started talking, he said he never wanted to become one of the guys I talked about who broke my heart, and the heartbreaking part is, he did. Did I participate in the breaking of my own heart? Sure, I probably should have put my foot down a long time ago and stood up for myself instead of always trying to accommodate him. I definitely should have taken things as they were instead of how they could have been. There are many things I could have done, but life is just a string of decisions that build out your story.

In August 2020, he was reassigned for work. Our relationship has been a rollercoaster since February, and I hate rollercoasters. One conversation we had in April has always stuck out to me, it was as though he wanted to be on the same page with me, but we were never going to get there.

I told him, "I still love you, but I really don't like you."

He responded, "I know, and I wish I could fix that."

I wish he wanted to fix it as badly as he seemed to want to at the time.

I told him, "In terms of standing points in my life, you already in the negative anyway. But if you wanted to work at it for real, that could change."

"You are too forgiving."

"I could be a petty bitch if I wanted to, but all that negativity doesn't serve me. What am I supposed to do? Continue to punish you forever. That's not right, let alone fair. Also, I'm not some basic girl you met on the street last week. Who said earning it would be easy?"

"Hmmmm. . . Alright, Nicole puts it down."

"I can when I need to. You're still on block one anyway."

"{Crying emoji} Block one? What's that?"

"The very beginning of the hole you said you're in. It's the bottom essentially."

"Ok. Ma'am."

"You said it. And you said I was too forgiving; you did this to yourself. Trust me, I want to see you succeed."

"Aight, I'm going to work on the comeback slowly but surely."

"I appreciate that. I used to like you so much better before. Lesson #1: actions speak louder than words."

"Oh, man. I know. . . It's sad to see how it all fell apart. Shame. Shame. Shame."

He left in May, and besides a single text response, I didn't hear from him until December. Honestly, that's only because I reached out to him. He had been my confidant and shoulder for so long that I didn't know where else to turn.

I know I titled this, "Ain't No Wrath. . ." so you may have expected yelling and ranting. I have already done that; it served no purpose. I asked questions and got called "complicated." So, I just stopped. Do you know how fucked up it is to feel that caring for someone is problematic? I made a promise, and I was going to move on.

For me, true defeat is when I stop putting in effort and when silence no longer bothers me. In the first few weeks, sure the questions surfaced and I wanted to reach out, but I stopped myself. I refuse to put myself back into a situation where I already had a pretty solid idea about the outcome. I slipped up one day at brunch but whatever. I can blame that on the mimosa. When he was radio silent for my birthday this year, that's when I truly knew it was a wrap. One thing we never did, no matter how mad or upset we were, was miss a birthday. It was the first time in five years he wasn't first. Talk about silence ringing loud and clear.

In a twist of fate, I let my silence speak for me. You are not going to be with me and be involved in my life in any capacity only when it's convenient for you.

At the time, maybe he was right that I am too forgiving. Maybe I love too much and too hard. I am ok with that. It doesn't make me extra, it doesn't make me complicated, it makes me who I am. My friends always try to encourage me to protect myself more, but I am really bad at it. This has always been my argument: I am not going to change who I am because you want to act like your mother did not raise you correctly. Funnily enough, I do have a breaking point, and me being nice to you is to save you from the raging bitch I know I can become. My personality has two speeds: nice and savage. There is no in between.

I know constantly leaning toward nice makes me suscep- tible to being hurt. I don't regret it, like I said previously. It taught me something. Yeah, I was heartbroken, but also my ego was just bruised. I had to be a big girl and move along. Two very important takeaways ladies and gentlemen. I have seen great men go through their own drama as well.

1. "Treat me like a joke, I promise you I'll leave like it's funny." It may take a few times, but I do learn eventually.
2. If you want me, you are going to have to put in the work to earn me.

After one of our weeks of not speaking, I wrote a piece on silence. There are always three sides to a story: yours, mine, and the truth. Here is one third of the puzzle.

# Silence by Nicole A. McKenzie

Silence—a place with no sound
Someone not speaking, we would say is silent
Someone telling you not to speak is silencing you
The theme is just to be quiet
But have you ever stopped and listened to the silent sounds?
Those nonverbal cues
The quiet behavior
The true meaning behind silence
A person can say so much and never utter a word
That choice to not answer that call
That decision to not pick up the phone and call
The thought of leaving that message on read
The moment of not writing a message at all
The blank stare in a conversation
The pulling away
The exit
Silence can heal and it can hurt
It can give you the peace and quiet you need to rummage
through your thoughts
Meditate
Let go of the negative
But it can also stifle
Make you feel alone
Trapped in the place with nowhere to go because there is no
sound to follow
No one reaching out to you, it's just silence
Externally it can show disinterest or just a shy personality
It can cause people to feel comfort or pain
Peace or confusion
So I want you to take a moment

*Take a second and wonder*
*Something so simple*
*What are you using your silence for?*

Just because I love him, doesn't mean I have to continue to hurt myself.

# PART IV

# NOW WHAT?

# INTIMACY VERSUS SEX

———

I have two vivid memories of the first time an adult started teaching me about sex. The first was church, where most of us learned the cardinal rule: don't have sex before marriage. No one ever really explained the intricacies of it, but they made sure to scare the hell out of you to make sure you did not participate in such acts. Well, at least they tried to.

The second was when a childhood friend of mine whom I did not interact with much got pregnant and my mom confronted me about whether or not my friends were having sex. Which to that question, I responded, NO! Even if they were, I didn't know about it.

I was so naive when I was young that it is truly laughable. For example, I never understood how people could say, "I don't know, it just happened." I would think to myself: *What do you mean it just happened?* To me, sex was such a big deal that hearing that "it just happened" as if you tripped and fell made no sense. Did you just trip into his bed and fall out of your clothes? Though, it's been said, experience is one of the best teachers you will ever have. One night in my college dorm, I found out exactly how one trips and falls into bed with someone, without any type of forethought. I finally understood how it could "just happen."

As I attempted to navigate the dating world, I always held close to my heart that I wanted to be seriously dating the person I would be intimately involved with. I usually just chalked it up to being emotional, I never quite understood what it was that was I after. All I knew was that I enjoyed the moments of just being with that person and feeling safe with them.

In 2017, about five months after Derrick and I stopped talking, I met this guy named Justin. Justin and I met online, talked for a few weeks, and went on one or two dates. It was all very low key. Early on he was very upfront about how he was just looking for something casual.

*For those of you fortunate enough to not know what that means, it's essentially boyfriend and girlfriend privileges without boyfriend and girlfriend expectations. You guys go out and are intimately involved, but neither of you owe the other anything.*

Against every bone in my body, I decided that was ok. Not because I was trying to please him or keep him around, but because I thought maybe I needed a change and was interested in trying something different. Clearly being invested in people was not working, so I thought: *How about I try a different approach? Huge mistake by the way.*

One night he came over with the intentions of practicing his massage skills for his physical therapy classes. We ended up practicing something physical in a different sense. While the sex was good, it did absolutely nothing for me. Something felt like it was missing, much like the Xbox controller that I let him borrow and never got back. I did get one thing out of the whole encounter with Justin: I learned to never go against my intuition again. I hate casual sex, or any kind of situation that would be considered casual. Not because I think something is wrong with it, on the contrary, live your best life. I actually admire people who can set aside their emotions with someone they are intimately involved with. Sometimes all I want to do is shut mine off. All mine do is hurt me or get me in trouble.

That off button, it's just not in my DNA, and I have learned to accept it and navigate my life in a way that works for me and my emotional self. You know how easy it would be if someone burned you, for you to just shrug it off like, "I was only here for the sex anyway." Not me, though. You would find me curled up in a ball tucked into the left side of my bed, eating a tub of Tonight Dough from Ben & Jerry's watching *The Great British Bake Off* attempting to make myself feel better and probably failing at it miserably.

I have reached this point in my life where I don't even want sex. Trust me, I can't believe I said that out loud either. It took me a while to figure out what I wanted. I had a general idea of course, we already addressed standards, but on a deeper level I was starting to understand the emotional energy that I was seeking as well. I would talk to people, attempt to entertain a conversation here or there, and it boiled down to this pattern that I kept experiencing. I am tired of men shoving unsolicited sex at me. If I want to sleep with you, trust me sir, I will let you know!

Could we hit pause for a second, actually get to know one another mentally before we jump the gun to physical? Spend time outside, go on random adventures, do a food tour of the city, get some ice cream, go to Top Golf, or have a Netflix marathon that isn't "Netflix and chill." Don't get me wrong, I'm not one to turn down a good cuddle. I just feel like things happen so fast that I miss out on getting to know someone on an emotional level, versus a relationship built on a physical level first. Not to say you can't sleep with someone on the first date and have a great relationship. That just isn't me.

Back when I liked Damien as a person, I asked him how he shows affection to someone he's involved with. I wanted to understand his vibes and mindset a bit more. He told me that he is the type of guy to get behind you, wrap his arms around your waist, kiss you right on the spot right below you ear as you two explore the grocery store. Or just kiss you on the forehead when he sees you busy doing work, just so you know he's there. I melted; my heart actually fluttered writing that.

That is the type of stuff that gets me. The small gestures, the little things that show you wanted to be connected with me one way or another. Goodness, I miss how he used to be when he used to act right. I want that, that feeling of want and need for a person. To me, that is why intimacy is so important. When you are having a bad day and want someone to lean on, a comforting arm can go so much further than the release sex offers.

Hey, Google, define intimacy.

"Emotional warmth or closeness."[33]

What I wanted finally had a word. I could at last express exactly what was important to me.

Intimacy is a feeling of warmth, feeling safe and secure in someone's arms. Knowing that I am mentally, physically, and emotionally safe. A kiss to the forehead, a long talk at two in the morning, an all-encompassing hug after a long day.

---

33  *Merriam-Webster.com Dictionary*, s.v. "intimacy," accessed January 28, 2021

That's intimacy to me, and I don't care if it's an unpopular opinion, but to me that beats out sex by a mile and a half. You can have sex with anyone, but intimacy is built with a special someone.

In the lovely year of 2020, it's the emotional connection that matters. If I were to be quarantined with you, I better like you on a personal level.

As I pen this out, it's been approximately twenty-seven years, six months, and twenty-six days since my last boyfriend. I know right, it's amazing I've survived in the game this long. If you're wondering, yes that means I've never had a boyfriend. Sure, I've talked to some people, maybe dated a few, but never quite got to popping that first question.

As I think back on the guys I have been involved with, I can see the similarities in the ones that I had a deeper connection with. The ones who offered me what I was looking for, when I did not even know what it was. With Kenny, he was a huge cuddler, which I loved. Physical touch is a big thing for me, it's one of the ways I show affection and like to receive it. Yes, it is one of my top three love languages.

Being cuddled makes me feel safe, subsequently invoking that sense of intimacy. At that time, I just knew that I liked being snuggled up and wrapped in someone's arms or just being randomly touched for no reason.

One night Kenny came over, but he wasn't acting like himself. He was very standoffish. My friend had invited us over to her place for a game night, and I convinced him to go hoping it would take his mind off what was upsetting him. I wanted his time with me to be that safe space where he could let go, you know? The walk to her place was silent, he barely spoke a word to me and just walked behind me. Once he got there, I guess it clicked that he at least had to pretend to enjoy himself, and after a while you could see his shoulders relax as we slipped back into our usual groove. We played card games all night, and I never moved from my spot in his lap. Eventually, we called it a night around one or two in the morning. We held hands when we walked back, and I sat on his lap on the ride back to my room. I was happy that I could offer him in abundance, so freely, what he offers me to make him feel better and create an enjoyable night for both of us.

Since Kenny, I have had one spark of an intimate relationship, and one that really rocked me to my core. I was transitioning through and out of this relationship that made me realize how much weight I put on emotional connections. It was one of those things that I knew in theory based off "dating" Kenny and Derrick, but with Damien, things were just so much deeper, and I was so out of my element that there was nothing to do but learn.

Stepping into my relationship with Derrick, in the time that we were together, Derrick and I had sex once. When I think back on our time together, that is not on the forefront of my mind and not because it wasn't good, because between you and I, it was phenomenal.

Memories of Derrick and me revolve around snuggling on his couch, my head in his lap while he runs random patterns up and down my arm while watching some action movie. He and I had busy work schedules, but we always put our best foot forward to see each other at least once a week outside of work. Dating him was a testament to how much I liked this man, because he lived an hour away from me by car, and taking the train was a pain in the ass. However, we did develop a nice system. I would come to him, and he would take me home. Whenever we were in the car together, he would always put his hand on my thigh. Those moments and times where I felt, at ease, safe, and wanted, that's what I hold dear to the time that we had together.

I haven't seen or spoken to Damien in a while. He still watches my Snapchat stories but doesn't know how to pick up a phone. Anyway. . . as I mentioned, writing this is triggering to our time together. For me, it's not triggering anger or hurt. It's triggering this longing to go back to that bubble we had. Having the ability to be vulnerable with someone again and knowing that no matter how bad things may have seemed, I had a person who was willing to hold my hand through it.

Work has been something special, and not in a good way recently, and many a night I have come home just wanting a hug and to be able to let go knowing someone would be there to catch me.

Back when he and I were actually in the same state, I was on the phone with him, expressing how I could really use a hug. We made plans to hang out later in the evening, and the minute I stepped out of the car, he pulled me into his arms and whispered in my ear, "Here is that hug you were asking for." It was one of those all-encompassing hugs where he has two arms wrapped securely around you. Now, I am short, so my arms are around the middle of his back, my head is in his chest, I can smell the scent of his cologne, and I just feel my whole body relax from head to toe. No physical activity required. That is what emotional connections do for me. It just makes everything better. I just snuggled closer, never wanting to leave.

Being that Damien and I were long-distance, it was the small things that kept us together. As complicated as our situation was, I knew we were not in it just for the physical aspects because we were talking for eight months before anything ever happened, and I saw him twice within those eight months. Things could have easily fizzled out, but even though we had our miscommunications, fights, and whatever else life threw at us, it was our emotional connection that kept us together before things started getting shaky on their own. Even now, I miss being able to just pick up the phone and FaceTime him. I miss being able to send him silly memes or pictures on Snapchat. I miss hearing his voice, and I miss the way he would hold my hand and then spin me around into his body, I just miss him.

While sex may not have a high-ranking number in my life, I won't pretend like it doesn't matter. I think sex when you have an intimate connection with someone makes the experience that much better. Sex is a vulnerable place to find yourself in, you are as exposed as you can ever be. Couple that with being able to expose yourself beyond the physical plane and sex becomes something beyond any typical measure. Intimacy doesn't have to stand alone and neither does sex; together they are just another aspect of your relationship.

I think we value intimacy and sex exclusively and mutually; we just need to know how they blend the two in our relationships.

Before we end, I want you to stop and think about what intimacy means to you. Take your time, no rush, these mimosas come with free refills. I shopped around for a few answers, so we could compare notes with some of my closest girlfriends, who are all in different relationship statuses. So, let's see if you resonate with any of the below.

**Angie**: I feel like intimacy is more than sex. It's more about the care you put into that person.

**Logan**: Intimacy to me doesn't mean sex but affection. A little touch, a kiss here and there. Just not in a creepy way, you know. It can even be when your eyes connect, and it just gives you that feeling. When you're both smiling at each other and start laughing.

**Alexa**: I think it has a lot of meanings. It can be physical, sexual, or emotional, but I think the key to a really strong and healthy relationship is having all of them. And sexual intimacy has both the physical and emotional aspect. So, they're all intertwined.

**Shauntell**: First thing that comes to mind is sex. But there's levels to that. There's sex and then intimate sex. Intimate sex signals a connection, an understanding of love between two persons. Respect between one another.

**Jasmine**: I'm the wrong person to ask, but my two cents would be that intimacy doesn't mean sex. You can be emotionally intimate, and also intimacy can just be a snuggle or kiss or something. Something that makes you feel close to the other person.

**Dani**: Intimacy to me is being comfortable with being completely vulnerable. At first thought I think sex, I think most folks do. You're naked, you offer yourself, you are at your most vulnerable. But one level deeper, there's the emotional vulnerability that makes it that much more. If I take that leap and let you into my deepest self, tell you things that you could turn around and use against me, that's even more vulnerable than sex. And if you take my vulnerability and you protect it, you respect it and understand it, now I can breathe and relax and feel safe. And I can share more, unencumbered by doubt. That's intimacy.

Do you see yourself in one of these answers, or do you have one all your own? Remember, unless you are trying to have babies, don't forget your precautions. I know that these adorable Instagram babies are having your ovaries on fire just like mine.

# ME VERSUS MY OVARIES

———

Who in the audience feels like society puts unrealistic pressures on women? Ok, I am looking around surveying. Alright, so everyone! Glad we could be in agreement.

When I turned twenty-five, I was beginning to feel as though I was not where I was supposed to be, and twenty-six, that was a different ball game. I thought I may have just hit rock bottom (dramatic I know, but it was how I felt). I was in a job I really did not like. I was battling the decision of whether to go to grad school or not to go to grad school. I had recently been rejected by an MBA prep program, and I didn't know if I still wanted to live in DC; nothing felt right that year.

Whenever someone asked me how it was going, or asked how I was doing, I'd always tell them I was just trying to get my life together.

For years, I talked about trying to get my life together and sometimes still utter this statement. As I think about this now, I wonder, what on Earth am I trying to get together. Shouldn't I be building and molding a life instead of trying to piece some figment of my imagination together, creating a societal definition of what my life should be looking like at this point?

I was a victim of pressure. The pressure of feeling as though I should have had it figured out by now. The pressure of feeling as though I have nothing to show for as much time has passed. The truth is, I'm twenty-seven and barely any time has passed. I have a job, an apartment, a whole bachelor's degree from Georgetown, and I really feel unaccomplished. I am writing a whole book for crying out loud. There is something very wrong here.

There is so much more to live for and discover in the world. Yes, I'm going to fall apart and yes, I am going to get back up. Yes, I am going to fail and yes, I am going to succeed. I mean, I have been laid off from two jobs in my life due to company acquisitions. I have been in corporate America for four years; someone explain how that's possible. The answer: life

The point is, I have had to learn to stay in my lane and realize that my lane is going to look different than those around me. So what that my mother was married and had me by the time she was my age? That doesn't mean I won't get married and have kids someday. I realized I had to stop succumbing to the fear that it wouldn't happen because of some unnecessary timeline I created in my head. This was another "list" that I needed to let go off. Whenever I think of clocks, besides being in a relationship, I have started to think about my biological clock as well. I have also wanted to be a mom on the younger end of the spectrum because I love the relationship my mom and I have. I wanted an age range like what we have for me and my children.

My aunt jokingly asked me once if I am going to give my grandfather great-grandkids and at this rate, the answer to that is going to be a no. I know I have time, lots of years before my clock becomes an issue, and with the miracles of science, even more time than before. There is the option of freezing your eggs. There are women who are freezing their eggs for a multitude of reasons. One of the reasons highlighted in an article by *Elanza Wellness*, "13 Legitimate Reasons Why Women Are Freezing Their Eggs," is that women have not found the right partner. Despite the rise in Single Mother children, the majority preference of women is still to raise a child with a life partner. Bonnie, who is thirty-eight, said, "It's not like I haven't been trying to find a decent guy to date. I'm just not willing to settle. For me, having kids is more about starting a family with the right person."[34]

Oh Bonnie, aren't we all just trying to find a decent guy to date in general?

Like many women, while I know I can have kids on my own, I do not want to. I want three kids. Right now, I am leaning two boys and a girl, but we will see what biology decides to do in the future. The idea of two big brothers and the baby sister warms my heart just thinking about it. I think my dad is a little over being the only guy in our little family. I just have this image of those three gorgeous chocolate babies, all snuggled in their blankets sound asleep, my husband and I watching them in the doorway. *Sigh.*

When people mention the option of having kids on my own, I tend to just stare at them. You ever just want to hit people for the things that come out of their mouth? It's not that they are wrong, it's just, they don't see the vision you are trying to create. Yes, I am aware I could have kids on

---

34 "13 Legitimate Reasons Why Women Are Freezing Their Eggs," *Elanza Wellness*, last updated May 12, 2020.

my own if I choose, but I want my vision, remember? The husband, nice house, and white picket fence I talked about earlier. I was raised in a solid family unit, and that is what I want. I want to have kids, not even just for me but for my future husband. I am a complete daddy's girl through and through. I want that for my daughter, to see her thriving with her dad doing all sorts of cute stuff. To watch my sons out back playing with their father. I want to plan a bomb Father's Day and have amazing Christmases together with our little family. If the time comes where that doesn't seem likely (the time isn't going to come because I am speaking my family into existence but for the sake of the hypothetical), I will cross that bridge when I get there.

The future that I want to build for myself makes dating a little complicated. I want to date someone who is not only open to having kids, but also is not trying to wait ten years to make that happen. I'm thinking four to five years, you know. Men and women are also waiting longer to start families, which is great. We are all out here enjoying dating, pursuing careers, and overall just enjoying life. The catch comes when women become interested in wanting to start that family but still can't find the right partner. In my earlier example, Bonnie was thirty-eight and still looking for the right partner. In the same article, they interviewed a guy named Joe who said, "Of course, I want to be a dad! Having a family has always been really important to me. I'm enjoying my life right now, dating and working hard. I just don't see the need to rush into anything."[35] So what is a woman like Bonnie supposed to do, keep waiting until she is forty-five? Regardless of

---

35  "13 Legitimate Reasons Why Women Are Freezing Their Eggs," *Elanza Wellness*, Last updated May 12, 2020.

whether you freeze your eggs or not, pregnancy itself comes with complications as you get older. That is a whole scientific conversation for later. Now we have a timeline conflict.

Angie and I went to brunch one afternoon with the Brunch Club, a group of us four girls who always do brunch together. Afterwards, we decided to get our nails done, but the salon had closed early. We ended up at a bar/lounge on U street. We ordered and just sat people watching, which in DC is one of my favorite activities—you can learn so much. About an hour in, this guy came and sat at a table across from us. He was placing a to-go order and asked us if the wings were good since that is what we had at our table. We shook our head in affirmation and went back to talking. I am not quite sure how we ended up in a full-blown conversation with him, but we did. He introduced himself as Adrian. He marveled us with his life story and, somehow, we ended up on the topic of dating. He mentioned how he was in this part of his life where school and work were his main two priorities, asserting that he was not boyfriend material, but he would make a good weekend boyfriend. *You know, at least he was honest.*

We asked, "Who do you date?"

"I tend to date women who were between twenty-two to twenty-five or women who were forty-five and up, because the rest in the middle are on a timeline that I do not have time for and are too much work," he replied, very matter of fact.

"Wow, I feel offended," I muttered under my breath.

He went on to explain that maybe when he is forty to forty-five, he will settle down. To him, I say live your best life. I would've chalked this up to a one-time occurrence if I had not heard this argument before. Society pushes women to have a family and be committed so much earlier, but it's ok for men to take their time. Who are these women supposed to be committed to then?

### ARE YOU THREATENED OR NAW?

I feel as though women sometimes get caught up in this unfortunate dichotomy of men either not being ready or men are scared. Being a successful woman is both a blessing and a curse. On one hand, you do not need a man to take care of you, but on the other, apparently some men find them intimidating. Why, I don't know, but I have been told success is threatening.

Question of the day, hour, or section, depending on where you left off:

Why are men intimidated by successful women?

We are going to quickly circle back to *Why Won't You Date Me?*, where Nicole Byer continues to bring the heat! In one episode called "Making a Polyamorous Relationship Work" with Deray Davis, a comedian with two girlfriends, Davis discusses his relationships and experiences. He says that he feels like a lot of men, himself included, are intimidated by successful women. He flat out said at 3:54 on the podcast that successful women make him uncomfortable.[36]

His reasoning being that he likes to be a provider and feels that women who fought to get to that place of success are in a different mental space. His money doesn't mean anything to these types of women. The Oprahs of the world and the Naomi Campbells. Rihanna cursing out her billionaire boyfriend on the boat. These women do not care about what

---

36   Nicole Byer and Deray Davis, "Making a Polyamorous Relationship Work," July 26, 2019 in *Why Won't You Date Me*, produced by HeadGum, podcast, MP3 Audio, 3:54.

is in his bank account, they expect more. Dating a woman who is powerful is harder because they can't be lied to or fed bullshit. Every man likes to bullshit, and it's just hard for them with an empowered woman. Besides your ability to provide, what else are you bringing to the table? Whereas, on the flip side, a woman who is not that successful would see Deray's success as prestige and would be willing (in theory) to deal with more.

I'm going to be rational (for all of five seconds) and say ok, I can see where he is coming from. He wants to be able to be a man's man and really adhere to those societal gender roles.

I am a woman who looks up to Auntie Riri as an idol. Come on, Fenty Beauty, Fenty Skin, Savage X Fenty, and FENTY! So, to Mr. Davis, how dare you? I'm calling full bullshit because frankly, y'all have got to GROW THE FUCK UP. You keep talking about being a "man," well be a man! You can't handle a woman having her own because now you have lost control. She doesn't need you in the way society has created you to be needed.

Then, he turns around to say something I have heard a million times before, which leads to my confusion about this situation. "I don't want a broke bitch either." Side note: we have to stop calling women bitches regardless of the situation, but that is a debate for another time.

Let me see if I understand. I have to be successful but not too successful because then I will be threatening your ego. I can compete, but I have to be competing with another woman for your attention and not my bank account? I can be sexy, but not too sexy because then I would be labeled a whore. *Lord, please be a fence.* Marinate on that for a second. . . yet people want to tell me the patriarchy isn't alive and well. Ha, it's like saying systemic racism isn't real.

A real man is not intimidated by how much money a woman makes or how successful she is. Ambition and success do not equate to whether she would be a good partner or a good mother. Shouldn't you be more worried about her personality, likes, and dislikes? The similarities of your goals instead of the differences in your power.

I understand if you want to take care of me and be a provider, that's fine, but why can't you take care of me/us if I am successful? What happens if you can't provide? We are going to have to struggle. No! I am going to have your back the way I would hope you would have mine. I want a man to feel like a king, and I will rock with you as your queen. You treat me right, and I'll treat you right. Let's go ahead and build this empire.

Not saying everyone is like this because on the flip side, I know guys who love a woman who can stand on their own, but I've also heard this story too many times to not address it.

One of my friends introduced me to her mentor. This woman is #goals. She is an entrepreneur, gives back to her community, and has a phenomenal job. Truly the definition of a woman who doesn't need a man to take care of her. She has a beautiful home, and for all intents and purposes, she is set. Only thing missing: a special someone in her life. One afternoon, we were talking about the development of this book and what dating is like, and she told me that she finds it hard to meet men who are not intimidated by her. Now, she is a few years older than me, and one would hope it would be easier, but nope! Different age, different set of problems. They see her home and car and automatically shy away.

This boggles my mind. The way I see it, all the man has to provide is his love and attention. Shouldn't having her own make the relationship easier? I don't think I ever realized how hard it can be for successful women to also find a partner until now.

Whitney Cummings has this joke: "You know what's a turn off for a man, owning a home."[37]

As much as it sucks, I am thankful that they are still looking and open to looking. I would never want them to shrink themselves just to sooth some man's ego. They, and all the boss women in the world, deserve so much better than that.

Women should not have to choose between wanting to be a wife and being successful. Gender roles have evolved, workplaces have evolved (well at least they are starting to), woman are making so much headway in the world that this archaic thinking of success being a bad thing is like a slap in the face. A woman should not be afraid to scream at the top of her lungs how amazing she is in fear of intimidating a man. My advice is this, do not shrink your crown to make it light enough for a man to hold, find a stronger man to hold you up, and wave as you stroll past those who tried to play you.

### BUT, WHAT ABOUT THEY ALREADY HAVE KIDS?

What about those men and women who already have kids? I have come across many profiles of men that straight up say they do not want to date a woman with kids. I am sure there are women who feel the same way about men. I do not see it as an ultimatum, just more of a preference. I would like to date someone who does not already have a child, but it is also not a make or break. It is a decision, though, that you have to really think about before you get too deeply involved with someone.

---

37  Nicole Byer and Whitney Cummings, "Emojis are a Red Flag," December 13, 2019, in *Why Won't You Date Me*, produced by HeadGum, podcast, MP3 Audio.

Derrick's son was four when we started dating. While we were not together long enough for me to have an impact on his son's life, his son did have an impact on our relationship. If I am dating someone who doesn't have a child, I can expect to be a priority. I can be disappointed if a date is cancelled and probably pout a little. However, when there is a child involved, they are always the priority, and it is something you have to adjust to. You don't really get to pull selfish cards in this situation. Dates can and will get canceled. Your level of understanding and care has to be notches above average.

We had dates that we had planned weeks in advance, but something would come up and we would have to reschedule. Sure, I was disappointed, but I needed to be understanding. He needed me to be understanding because his first job was to be a dad. Mind you, Derrick did not have full custody of his son; that is another level of prioritization and developing your role in that relationship.

I know that right in this moment, I am not in a position to have kids. I do think about it though. My revisions editor did make a very good point: "No one is ever READY for kids, they come when they do, and you fill that role when it happens. You'll never have enough money, space, time, or diapers. But I can tell, you, will always have more than enough love." Isn't love all we want?

Do I want to plan having kids to the best of my ability? I get it life is full of many, many surprises and sometimes things just don't work out the way you think they should. However, I want to give my child the best that I can offer them, and for me right now, the only way I could do that is by attempting to plan as many of those factors that I mentioned as possible. In the meantime, I get to play auntie to my little nephew (yes, I know I am an only child, but I have pretty much adopted my closest friends into my family, so their kids became my nieces and nephews) and buy him outfits and gifts to my heart's content!

# DATING AS A
# CHOCOLATE GIRL

———

As I mentioned in the introduction of this book, one of my biggest reasons for writing this was just to be open and vulnerable and to let people recognize that it's ok to feel hurt and upset when things do not work out. Process the emotions. It's ok to be frustrated we have to get all that out and learn from it to finally be able to heal and turn a new life into something better and brighter, but we can't do that if we don't learn from what we have been through.

In the spirit of vulnerability, it wouldn't be right if I didn't address this topic. I am writing this book as a young Black woman. A lot of times, Black women don't get the opportunity to express their frustrations in life, let alone dating. We are either being too picky or too mouthy. If we have a problem, we are too loud or aggressive. I just wish that before people jumped to judgments, they would just stop and listen.

Some of you may already have an idea of where this is going, and I don't need all of the *oh god she is going to talk about white women dating Black men isn't she* comments.

Why, yes I am, you are not wrong. But you see that same energy that you have of *oh my God*, I'm allowed to have the same energy. **PSA: You can love who you love, I am not here to judge your decisions, I am here to speak on my experience. I just want the love to be rooted in the right reasons.** I live for love, it's part of my Pisces ideology. It doesn't matter who you find it in, once it's real and pure and energizes both of you up honey, I could care less about the color of skin.

My issue is how Black men are a fetish and how some— and keyword here, *some*—of them have let this attention go to their head and all of sudden I'm not worth a dime.

My issue is how some Black men have decided that Black women are not good enough anymore. If they are seeking success, they need to be with someone of a lighter complexion.

Hold on, isn't your mom Black?

Isn't your sister Black?

Your aunt, cousin, all the women in your family?

If I am not your cup of tea, you can just say that, but do not insult me and any woman you come across because I'm not your "shade."

I don't know when this happened, but it's everywhere: the bashing, and side-eye of it all just exploded out of nowhere. I would see reckless things on Instagram and read posts on Twitter alluding to statements that made it seem like Black women needed to step their game up because white women were coming for their spot. I have heard rappers on the radio saying reckless things such as how white women are learning to fry chicken, so Black women need to watch out.

Are you kidding me right now? I am sorry, I didn't realize that my value to you was built into my ability to fry chicken and the size of my ass. I've never actually fried chicken a day in my life. So, I guess I'm not worth much regardless. Also, someone cannot come for a spot that was mine to start with. I wish you could see how hard I just rolled my eyes.

These are things that drive me crazy about dating and makes navigating this such an emotional mess. I've read profiles where people write things like "Sorry I only date Hispanic girls or white girls" but will have the nerve to end it with, "but I'm open to anyone with a good conversation." Sir, I do not want to have a conversation with you, date who you like, it's ok.

I have had someone tell me once "I usually don't date dark-skinned women, but you're different."

No, no, no. I'm not going to be your trial and error. I'm not gonna be your learning tool about how you now feel about my sisters as a whole. Absolutely not. Please check yourself at the door, sir. I am done with the bullshit statements of "Oh you're cute for a Black girl." This is the stuff that happens every day, and no one wants to talk about it. Should I just be happy that you think I am "cute"? We are the ones literally keeping this race alive, and some of you do not care. The discussion never really gets the right attention it deserves. We just get labeled as judgmental.

Right after Harry and Meghan's interview was released, we all know that Twitter went wild, but one tweet stuck with me in particular. "The fact that Black women are praying they find a Black man that protects them, the way Harry protects Meghan REALLY says a lot."[38] This resonated with me so much, because that is it, that is all we want. Someone who is going to protect us and take care of us the way we

---

38  Count Your Blessings Yt Girl (@LilHeffeBarbie), "The fact that Black women are praying they find a Black man that protects them, the way Harry protects Meghan REALLY says a lot," Twitter, accessed March 9, 2021, 12:03 p.m.

have been protecting and taking care of others our whole life. Black women are scarred but still try to fight each and every day. My mom told me a story of this couple she read about a few weeks before this interview. A young Black couple had been married for over eighteen years. They had two children together, and she helped him build his career. As a true Black queen, she was the foundation of her household. Beautiful story right. . . well things took a turn, and he divorced his wife, married a younger Caucasian woman, and they had three kids together. He barely has communication with his kids from his first marriage. Tends to go on as though they barely exist.

Let that resonate with you for a second. . . Do you still think Black women don't have a right to be angry? Nothing about the story is new; happens all the time. It is as though we are only good enough to get you to the goal line, but we do not deserve the celebration for the hard work that was put forth.

In developing the theme of "The List Has to Go," my lovely development editor Elissa brought up the story of Mark Ruffalo. He and his wife have been together since way before his big screen roles, back when he had nothing, and she loved him as he was. They grew together as a couple and are still going strong in his newfound wealth and position. I love these stories; I just wish they translated into my world. But, more often than not, a young Black couple in that same position, that rider of a woman, can easily find herself being left for a white woman. I mean Kanye said it in one of his songs and then ended up following through. It is as though they get a taste of success and need to "upgrade" the woman they are with. Last time I checked, women like

Michelle Obama were worth their weight in gold, diamonds, and rubies. Something to think about.

When I was young, I wanted nothing more than to be caramel. I wanted to be lighter so bad, y'all. I thought if I was lighter, guys would think I was cute. It's wild how strong colorism is and to this day, people want to act like it's not. I witness this with my own eyes, and it's broken me down before, I'll admit it. But I realized I couldn't stay down, I had to stand up for me and all the dark chocolate girls out there.

I am beautiful, and I am popping. I am Black and confident, impressively dripping in Black beauty, elaborately infused with melanin, extravagantly bathed in chocolate, like our girl Lupita! Lupita is chocolate woman goals. Honestly, she is just a goal in general. I also knew I had to love myself for my future kids. I want them to love themselves as much I know I'll love them, regardless of their complexion. No man's salty words shall prosper.

In conclusion, if you don't like me and my melanin, fine, but I would like to remind you it's the same melanin you have in your skin. You don't have to like me, but what you will do is respect me. Black men have been through a lot—the world literally tries to annihilate them, and I stand behind them because I know how important they are. I will always fight for you; my dad is a Black man, my grandfather, my cousin, my best friend, and I love them all dearly. I'm always going to fight for their lives and do what needs to be done to protect them.

My wish is that some of you would see how even though you have tried to tarnish us we still stand for you and try to protect you. I wish you would give us the damn credit we deserve. We can, because we have done it for centuries, but it would be nice to not have to continue to fight this battle alone.

# IF WINNIE THE POOH CAN WEAR A CROP TOP, I CAN TOO!

———

This topic is very dear to my heart because I have struggled with body image issues my whole life. I have days when I feel cute and think I look good, then I have days where I think to myself, this in the mirror is not *it*. With quarantine, things got out of hand, and this is exactly why I do not keep snacks in my house.

The notion that people who do not fit into society's depiction of healthy are lazy is completely false. The crazy thing is, I am a gym fanatic. I love working out. During quarantine, I was going stir crazy not being to work out the way I normally do. Before I started going to Bash in 2018 like I mentioned, I went to a studio called Orangetheory and held unlimited packages for both studios. I was in class at least four to five times a week, sometimes six if I was really doing the most that week. The gym became my happy place, seeing how fast I could run, how heavy I could lift. Even though I went through all these awesome body changes, I never really felt fully comfortable with my body. I would get to this point of peak fitness and then something would happen that would knock me back again. It felt as though I could never get past that point.

I have struggled with my body since I was in middle school, and always being that chubby kid eventually led to an amazing glow up after I graduated college. This is when I discovered the joys of strength training and have been hooked since. It wasn't an easy route though, as I have a joke with my best friend since third grade, who is practically my twin, that we have been dieting our entire lives, even now.

The journey of loving my body has been an interesting ride. Even now, there are days where I can fully embrace it and days where I feel like I shouldn't eat food. While not a constant battle the way it used to be, sometimes old insecurities can rear their heads.

Most of my friends are smaller than I am, and most of them are what society considers a normal, conventional beauty size and I have never been that that a day in my life. It's an interesting mental dichotomy because they all wish they had my work ethic to get to the gym. To me, that's mind-blowing, because the gym is the easy part. I have spent so long looking up to them, wishing I could be what they are. The fact that they are looking up to me, at what I'm doing for my body, was so *bleh;* my brain did not compute.

I am one of those women that are blessed with a very proportional body. I look a lot smaller than the weight on the scale, which honestly in my journey has caused me the biggest headache. Growing up, all you learn is about your BMI and if you are this tall, you should weigh this much. That is a load of bullshit, but I digress. I am 5'4" and I am never going to weigh 120 pounds, and I am ok with that!

I have never wished for abs; all I have ever wanted was a flat stomach and lean arms. Before someone tries to tell me that you cannot lose weight in one specific part of your body, I am aware of that. However, after the overall slim down, those are the areas I would most like to target. My trainer is more than a trainer—she is the big sister I did not know I needed. She is just as passionate about mental health as she is about physical health. She teaches me every day about giving yourself grace, recognizing when your body needs rest, and most importantly that this journey is not a sprint, it's just your life journey. You will have days where you kick ass and days where all you want to do is sit on your ass, and both options are perfectly fine.

Like many of my friends, she jokes that she wishes she had an ass like mine and every time anyone says this, I just laugh and always say the same thing: if I could trade you half of this behind just to get that physique, then girl take it, please I'll still be good. Right behind my smile, my booty is my next best physical attribute. I am proud of it though; I do a lot of squats and lunges to maintain the lift.

I know I am not a "traditional" beauty, and from experience, I am usually not the girl that guys gravitate toward. I am the girl that they meet on accident and strike up a conversation with, then realize I am a cool person. Not the one that they break their necks going around the corner for a second and third look. Let's be real with one another, we all want to be noticed and receive just a little attention, especially if you are still out in these streets hoping to find someone. Feeling like being a wallflower, being approached in spite of something, learning to combat what society thinks about you carrying that emotional baggage, is exhausting. That feeling fuels the questions. Am I not pretty enough? Am I not small enough? What is it that is going wrong? This eventually leads to the bigger question I have had for myself: why won't they date me?

This question also happens to be the title of one of my favorite podcasts with Nicole Byer. If you ever need a pick me up, I 10/10 recommend *Why Won't You Date Me?*[39]

Her content is both juicy and informative, and honestly what more could you ask for? A few weeks ago, she did a segment with author Roxane Gay called "Fatphobia." She addressed two topics that hit the nail on the head at the intersection of weight and dating.

1. "Men will date her, in spite of her weight. Meaning, they are attracted to her personality so they can overlook the weight.

2. Men will want to sleep with her but not actually date her."[2]

To the first point, have you ever had someone give you a compliment that sounded like a backwards insult? That is how I feel about this. Some people date purely for the physical, I call that hooking up, but whatever, to each their own. Others' primary goal in dating is an emotional connection. While I tend to lean to the latter, I would be a fool to not acknowledge that physical attraction plays a role in wanting to date someone. I truly think that if you don't find your partner attractive, the chemistry in your relationship is going to be off. As cheesy as it sounds, I want to be able to look at him and be like damn, that's mine, and for him to be able to do the same. Everyone's attraction is different, someone I'm attracted to might not be the same for someone else, which is perfectly fine. I want us to find each other appealing.

39 Nicole Byer, December 2017, in *Why Won't You Date Me*, produced by HeadGum (2017–2021) and Team Coco (2021–Present), podcast, MP3 Audio.

Knowing your partner has something that they so blatantly don't desire about you, such as your weight, is a recipe for a mental disaster. I am fortunate enough to not have to have dealt with a relationship like this, but I can just imagine the mental toll. Even with the two guys that I dated who appreciated my body and my curves, I still had my own reservations about myself in comparison to them.

I know I have not been explicit in physical details about the men that I have been involved with, but I do have a type. Six-foot tall, athletic build, and a killer smile. The trifecta to ruin your life, honestly. Derrick worked for Sysco—his whole job was a daily workout. He was lean but well built. Damien, his biceps alone made me dizzy.

I remember at the time being so consistent with going to the gym and making sure I was eating right. It wasn't necessarily a conscious decision; I just remember thinking I want to look good on his arm. This is not a bad thing if I am doing it for myself, but in this case I wasn't. I was doing it to fulfill some purpose when in these relationships. In a way, I was trying to prove that I was good enough to be with both of these men. This is ridiculous because according to my doctor, I am perfectly healthy. It is interesting how we can unconsciously change ourselves for others, without even recognizing that we are doing it.

As an individual who has been up and down with my weight my whole life, I have to want it for me for it to work. I can't want it for anyone else.

To the man who is out there thinking that just because you decided to look past her weight you are doing her a favor:

1. Goodbye!
2. You clearly need to get your priorities together.

She is going to be a queen with or without you, and right now I am voting without!

To Roxane's second point, I say this: If I'm good enough for a 2 a.m. phone call, but not good enough for a 2 p.m. lunch date, where people can actually see you, well then. . . fuck you! As a young woman who has battled her own insecurities, it is very easy to turn this into a me issue, when in reality it is a him issue.

This is a classic case of having to know your worth. You deserve to be seen and shown off. Being caught in an unhealthy situation like this can lead to a downward spiral of trying to force your body to change faster than it needs to or having thoughts such as, *Well at least I have his attention, and if he won't take me out, what makes me think someone else will?*

Roxane stated that someone once told her to "be grateful for any attention that she received"[40] and unfortunately, she bought into that botched thinking. She allowed herself, for a time, to be mistreated until she reached her breaking point. Regardless of the situation, man or woman, we all have a breaking point. She used hers to break free of the stigmas and the lies. Either you love me morning, noon, and night or you do not love me at all. I refuse to be a fetish to you; that is how this comes off. As though being with someone who isn't "thin" is socially unacceptable. Again. . . Goodbye!

The latest body trend was being slim thick: small in all the right places and thick in others. However, not everyone's body chemistry is made up that way! We are not all Meg Thee Stallion, who is 5'10". There are so many factors that play into

---

40  Nicole Byer and Roxane Gay, "Fatphobia", August 7, 2020, in *Why Won't You Date Me*, produced by HeadGum (2017–2021) and Team Coco (2021–Present), podcast, MP3 audio.

how weight will sit on a person. Back in 2018 when Auntie Riri gave us curves for days, she said in a *People* magazine article that she was thicc now and shot down anyone who tried to call her fat. In that article, she said one of my favorite quotes: "It comes with a price. You want to have a butt, you have a gut."[41] It is basic math people: if you do not weigh anything, you can't have anything.

2020 was a year of many firsts for me. One being I actually breached the subject of dating with some of my male friends. One in particular has always been my gym competition, which we are super competitive about. During quarantine, we gained some weight and he called me out about it. That's cool, time to put down the sugar. Then, two weeks later when we had our little dating chat, he told me how men are visual creatures. Whereas women will let a guy's personality lead them, a man will start with a woman's looks and go from there. It's best to put your best foot forward. While he isn't wrong, I appreciate the tough love, it's the fact that it's even a thing. *Sigh.*

Cue me going to throw out everything I like in my fridge. I don't keep snacks in my house or cookies or even ice cream. I do that so I won't eat it.

As much as I understand this point, when I work out, it's more for my health and mental health, than the aesthetics of it all. Let us not kid ourselves—I do very much have aesthetic goals, but mental health first, aesthetics second. Anyway, do I really want to be with someone who is going to judge me based on an unhealthy stigma of what the media has labeled healthy? No, no I don't. I want someone who will be my

---

41   Beatrice Hazlehurst, "Rihanna: You Want to Have a Butt, Then You Have a Gut'," *Paper,* June 15, 2020

gym partner, not some individual telling me to work out, as though I do not already have an unlimited membership at a studio. "**Our society has decided, without warrant, that women of all shapes, curves, and edges shouldn't feel good about their form**."[42] We need to advocate for change in thinking.

On Sunday, October 18, 2020 I had a bad mental day. I decided to go for a walk instead of wallowing in my bed. I had something very unexpected happen. I like to think of it as a divine intervention, if you will. I had a friend of mine text me completely out of the blue. He sent a simple text: "You ok. . ." I hadn't talked to anyone about anything being wrong and he and I hadn't talked in days. When I read this message, I was shook. I was prepared to try and handle this day on my own, and my fingers began to type, "I'm fine." Somewhere between the "F" and "I," something stopped me. Instead of hiding behind my go-to statement, I decided to accept the help I was clearly sent. Now I didn't have to do this on my own, the rest of the conversation goes like this.

"I don't know whether to be relieved or concerned. . . It has been a bad mental day. I felt really alone and like, unworthy."

"It's gonna be a constant thing in this current society. Gratification is so easy to get now, so people do anything for it.

Social media's created fake happiness, and in turn, that affects everybody else who can't have that level of false satisfaction.

---

42   Mary Nunes, "It's True: The Average Size of the American Woman Is No Longer 14," *Byrdie*, December 22, 2020.

You're writing books, not a lot of people can even put words into a text, so give yourself some credit. Don't let me start hitting you with the Melanin Queen vibes now."

*Have I mentioned how much I love this kid?*

"I was just having a moment. I was talking to someone and they insinuated that since men are visual creatures, I should probably lay low on the sugar. Which I get, but also, it's annoying."

*Please excuse his language, he is very passionate.*

"Fuck them! Shit, if they don't want you for you, then they don't need you when you glow up. Fuck him with his messed-up advice. Don't change to suit NOBODY!!! Cause, I know you already, what happens when you change, and they're still not satisfied? You gonna keep changing until THEY feel happy? When you gonna be happy?"

*When am I going to be happy?*

He is right. I've always striven to love everyone else and be there for other people, but when am I going to give myself grace, forgive myself for not loving me enough, and be proud of myself? Everyone else is, so why can't I see myself in the mirror?

This chapter is dedicated to girls like me. If you have ever had an ounce of doubt as to how much you matter, if you've looked in the mirror and can't see what I see, then I want you to know: "Sexy is not a size. Every calorie is not a war. Your body is not a battleground. Your value is not measured in pounds. You are just as fucking beautiful as any other woman."[43]

---

43   Holly Bross, "100 Quotes Ideas: Quotes, Inspirational Quotes, Me Quotes," Pinterest, December 4, 2018.

It'll be about springtime, inching to summer, by the time the masses get a hold of this book, and I just want to remind you that, "If Winnie the Pooh can wear a crop top, thrive in that crop top, sis." So, grab your shorts, bikini, summer dresses, whatever you want, and enjoy the body you are in. I know someone out there is going to love your cakes, just the way they are, boo!

*Siri, play* Birthday Cake *by Rihanna.*

# QTNA: QUESTIONS THAT NEED ANSWERS

———

QTNA: Questions that need answers is a phrase I probably use every day. As you have come to learn on this journey with me, I have way more questions than answers when it comes to dating, relationships and everything in between. As we will soon finish up our last pitcher of mimosas together, there are a just a few more things I would like to touch on.

- The confusing situations of life that make no sense, such as why is it when you are single your phone is full of tumble weeds, but the minute you really click with someone, suddenly, your exes become very apologetic and want to just make sure you are alright?
- Do you guys remember that show *Kids Say the Darndest Things*? I want to revamp this show. Coming fall 2021: *Men Say the Darndest Things.*
- Why, why do men do such things. . .

Full disclosure if you are a guy reading this and any of this offends you, then I am sorry that I am not sorry. If you are reading this and none of this applies to you, then sir, have a good laugh and tell Mr. In His Feelings that it's going to be ok. This is a safe space and it's not intended to be malicious.

Grab your glass, it is time for our last refill!

## #CONFUSION

Life is confusing, and since dating is part of life, then by extension, I think any situation involving men and women can lead to a confusing moment. Has this ever happened to you? Since COVID began, I have been living in leggings and sweaters, and honestly pre-COVID, it was much of the same. I just now have more leggings. On a day you decide to do the most, you can travel all over the city and see no one. However, the times you decide to throw on some sweatpants and a hat to run and get ice cream from the grocery store, you run past the man you want to make Mr. Right Now.

Why is it that when you see the most attractive men, you always feel or look the most unattractive? I know that I am cute, but I come in varieties. Nicole fresh out of Bash, bun barely hanging on, edges non-existent from the sheer humidity in our studio and just screaming for a shower is different than Nikki who just stepped out the house looking like a fun sized pack of M&Ms. She had her hair laid to the best of her ability (depending on the day), she has had a shower, and at the bare minimum she has her earrings in. We all know when you first meet someone, you are not meeting them, you are meeting their representative, and Nicole is not who I want to be leading the presentation, at least not right now.

Unfortunately for me, a few weeks ago, Nikki clocked out early and didn't tell anyone. As I was slowly making my way down the hill from a treacherous Endurance Day at Bash,

I decided, as much as I would love to go home and eat ice cream, I should probably go get a salad and eat some protein. My favorite salad spot in DC is Chop't. I know, I am such a millennial; salad shops and avocado toast, all things I could make at home but don't want to.

I made it down the hill, and as I approached the shop, I saw a gorgeous black Porsche sitting on the curb. DC is full of people with money, so I didn't think much of it, but I can appreciate some fine German engineering. To my surprise, and fear, the fine engineering had a fine driver as well.

Discreetly behind my glasses and mask, I checked him out. When my brain finally kicked back in as I stood behind him, I could do nothing but want to hide.

*Seriously, I went out last week looking like a whole meal— forget a snack—and I saw no one, but today when all I am trying to do is get some food and dip, this man has the audacity to grace my presence.*

My fake reality was shattered when I realized he was ordering food for him and his girlfriend. However, this didn't stop me from appreciating his genetics and time in the gym. As I stood there, failing at being discreet, I realized there was something very familiar about him. Then it hit me like a freight train. I went to school with this man. The only bright side was he probably doesn't remember who I am, so I can slowly disappear.

Regardless of his relationship status, situations like this as a whole are not right. There are women who leave the gym looking like they have just arrived—it's like they don't even sweat. I, on the other hand, look like I just got into a fight, but definitely won! As I walked out, salad in one hand, water in the other, I thought to myself, *If you don't love me at my*

*2007 Britney Spears, then you don't deserve me at my Beyon-cé.*[44] Whether it is sweatpants to the grocery store, pajamas to the hair salon, or exiting the gym, rock your "sweatpants, hair tied, I don't give a damn" look to your fullest. But don't forget to stunt on them every once in a while, you have to remind these folks who you are!

However, there are some folks who never need to be reminded of who you are because they lost that privilege a while ago. This situation comes in one of two ways:

1. Single with no attention; in a relationship all of your exes suddenly remember who you are.
2. Single with no attention,; in a relationship men in general just want to talk to you and "be your friend."

It's almost like a bizarre *Star Wars* moment. The moment you move on and have someone else, it's as though a bizarre force pushes them to your contact. "Hmmm, there is a disturbance, she is not thinking about me anymore—well can't have that happening."

You know what I say to the message, "Hey, it's been a while?"

"Who this?"

I truly believe this whole phenomenon is an offshoot of things happen when you least expect it. When you are single, that is when you expect people to be checking for you, because you are available, not the other way around. It is always shocking when you become unavailable that people now want to talk to you. I guess it furthers the expression that people always want what they can't have.

---

44  Candice Jalili, "'If You Don't Love Me at My' Memes Are Taking Over Twitter & I'm Pee-Laughing," *Elite Daily*, April 4, 2018

Now, I personally have not been in this situation; one of the few blessings of being "single" for twenty-eight years. However, I have heard the stories. My personal favorite, I like to call it out of the woodwork. I have a friend; her name is Ari. Ari dated this guy for a few years and a little over two years ago they broke up. In the past two years she has been playing the field, having fun, essentially living her best life. Recently, within the last few months, she has been steady with this one guy who we shall call James. Technically she and James are not together, heck they aren't even exclusive, but they have defined a relationship together that works for them. I mention her being steady with James for a reason. Before James, when she split with someone, that was the end because they were casual. What did it matter? She'd never talk to them again and they would disappear, out of sight out of mind. However, a few months after she and James became their version of an item, these guys from the past just started hitting her up, out of nowhere. I mean nowhere. I heard names that I hadn't thought to think of in over a year. Here is the kicker, they all happened in the same week. I wish I could admit I was making this up for content's sake. Honestly, I am not. I just kept asking, what was in the water that week? Some of these men don't even live in the same state anymore.

I understand, I will probably never be any less confused by these occurrences. However, I know it's not just me who deals with these things or hears of them. We are riddled with confusion every day. You know what else confuses me? Some of the things that come out of some guys' mouths.

## UNNECESSARY STATEMENTS

Has this ever happened to you? You see a guy, and he is just so handsome. You start hitting your friend next to you while trying to discreetly point him out before he moves out of your line of sight. You ever have him come up to you, and you sort of have to brace yourself, like yes, he is coming this way, maybe I can charm him. As you are getting your words together, he opens his mouth, and your whole fantasy about him comes crashing down.

*Sigh.*

Yeah girl, I've been there, too.

Some of the things I have heard coming out of you guys' mouth (yes, boys, men, young men, whatever you would prefer to be addressed as, I am talking directly to you) just makes me have to bow my head in actual desperation. As the girl on the receiving end, I can't even comprehend what came out your mouth, and truthfully most of it is unnecessary.

Some unnecessary statements include: "Is that ass real?" Technically this is a question, but that is beside the point. This question comes courtesy of a friend of mine who was on a first date.

Sir, I know you are not deadass right now. What is she supposed to think of you when this is one of your leading questions? Any of you have an answer in defense of one of your own? To add insult to injury, he later asked her if she was exotic. Excuse me, but what is she, a piece of fruit? What does exotic even mean anyway, we are all human, so maybe you should just travel more, and seeing someone who is mixed won't astound you so much.

Unnecessary statements also include contradictory statements. I have a friend Cassie who has been seeing a guy named Ryan for almost a year. While both are not ready for a committed relationship, they enjoy spending time together and building their own version of a relationship much like Ari and James did.

Many couples, regardless of where a relationship is headed, can find themselves in situations where the relationship seems off balance. Most times it happens in expectations, you expect them to be doing one thing but instead they are off doing another. In Cassie and Ryan's case, Ryan felt that she wasn't being vulnerable enough, that she was holding herself back and not being as invested in the relationship as he was. At first, she was taken aback but came to recognize that yes, her walls were up, and there was indeed space.

She took the conversation to heart and proactively tried to be more involved and open to him. You would think problem solved, right?

Not a chance, sis! If it were that easy, this book wouldn't exist.

Not even a week later, she is hanging out with him as she was getting ready to leave, she asked when they were going to see each other again. They both have demanding jobs, so finding time to spend with one another takes effort. His response to her question was:

"I think maybe we should see each other less."

. . .

What! Is this not the same person who was accusing her of lacking in the relationship? And now that she is putting in effort, he wants to backpedal. What is someone even supposed to do with that? Cassie didn't talk to him for almost a week after that. He did eventually also backpedal that statement and things blew over. Can you imagine starting to really bare yourself to someone, at their request, and then they just flip the script on you? You wonder why walls are built so high up.

Finally, my personal favorite, cliché, unnecessary statements are:

*It's not you, it me.*

and

*I miss you.*

It's not you, it's me. It's like a bad echo in a hollow room. Please stop. This is one of the more overplayed statements in the world. Worse than when they wouldn't stop playing the same song all summer. Now this, this I have had a front seat to numerous times in my life. I think I have about three more glasses left in this final pitcher, and I am going to need a whole one to get through these gentlemen.

Besides Jonathan, Derrick was the only other person I dated for any substantial amount of time. As you know, he and I didn't work out, and I would be a liar if I said it didn't hurt me. He was the first guy after Jonathan who I really had a vested interest in. Due to my helpless romanticism, getting over him was hard. After a few tears and weeks of healing, I was better. I saw him a few times at work, and I no longer had that nagging feeling of wanting to drop kick him and hug him all at the same time. Eventually, he disappeared. I didn't hear from him. I didn't see him. Derrick was truly out of my life.

Until. . .

About six months later, when a good day at brunch and a post-brunch roaming of DC led to an accidental, but interesting conversation. I am not one those people who deletes contacts if someone and I stop speaking. I just gradually let our text thread fall into the abyss. On this particular Sunday, I started typing Der in the search box because I was a little too inebriated to search for Derrell's name, and I only got to the "Der" and tapped the first name I saw. Too bad it was Derrick and not Derrell. Now expecting it to be a response from my friend, I happily pulled my phone out of my pocket and was met with the wildest shock it almost made me sober. Derrick had texted me back. I mean, the conversation was pretty boring, full of mostly pleasantries and inquiries into time passed. I think I was too stunned by his reappearance to realize he had actually reappeared. At the end of that, he asked to see me, and I agreed. Why, I don't know. Probably mostly out of curiosity. We all know my curiosity gets me in trouble.

Fast forward, we never actually saw each other, but that's ok because it just brings us to the best part. He texted me to ask what happened to us seeing each other. I told him I never received a call from him, so I figured nothing was happening. Turns out he did call, I just never got it.

As we talked, things got interesting.

"Did you want to reschedule or something?"

"Of course we can."

"For when?"

"What you think?"

"You're the one with the unpredictable schedule, unless that changed."

*Some days he had to be at work at 5 a.m., some days it was midnight, neither of us really ever knew when he would be called in.*

"Nope, still the same."

*A few seconds go by, and the bubbles start again, indicating he was typing. I received this unnecessary bombshell.*

"I miss you tho. . . a lot"

*No, no sir. No, you do not.*

"You miss me or getting free cupcakes every week?"
*Yes, I am a cheeky one when I want to be.*
"Girl, I miss you. . . The cupcakes were just a plus."

I would be a liar if I said he didn't get to me. However, that lasted about 2.65 seconds, until I remembered how we got to this conversation. I didn't mention how we stopped talking before because that wasn't the point I was trying to make. Here though, we can talk about it.

About three weeks before we stopped talking, I asked him what he was looking for because I just needed some clarity on what it is we were doing. He said he wasn't looking for a relationship right now. At the time, I was ok with that. Then three weeks later he hits me with the. . .

"It's not you, it's me."

In this time frame, he had met another girl and decided to pursue a relationship with her. Funny, I thought you weren't looking for a relationship. Now, I don't want to sound like a bitch, but that is why six months later when he came to me with the "I miss you," all I could think was: *What the fuck? I can't.* Why bother saying this when you and I both know nothing is going to happen because drum roll. . . you are still dating that woman you stopped talking to me for.

We could have just had a normal conversation and left the "I miss you" at home. I never saw him, and after maybe a few more days of basic chit chat, I never heard from him again.

This is a real throwback, but still of value to the story. A guy I really liked in high school didn't really give me the time of day, and seventeen-year-old Nicole was heartbroken. However, he and I have been Facebook friends since high school. In 2018, I went to Jamaica and posted some fire photos. Out of the blue, here he comes almost eight years later, talking about "hey bubbles" (that was my nickname back then).

I have to pause because this right here was a real-life example of one of my favorite IG quotes: "Ladies, no one will care more about your well-being than a guy you haven't heard from in months responding to your new swimsuit posts."[45] That's exactly what he did. We did a quick catch up, he told me about his kids, I told him about my uninteresting love life, and from there he decided to go down memory lane and inform me that he didn't pursue me when we were younger because he would have, and I quote, "destroyed me."

I know we all do dumb things as teenagers, but I think destroyed is a little much for an eighteen-year-old, don't you think? Also, almost ten years later, what am I supposed to say to that. . . thank you?

So what, we fast forward to now, what is this new information supposed to do? Why, just why, oh why? Not for nothing, it would have been my choice to decide whether I allowed you to destroy me or not. I had a pretty straight head on my shoulders as a kid, maybe I would have kicked you to the curb eventually, you don't know.

Men at times think we don't understand them, and that is very true, but in our defense some of the things they say are completely bonkers, and I for one have no better response than to look at you sideways.

I am sure that any girl at this current chapter can think of at least five reckless things a man has said to her that she had to stop and re-center herself before she could even think about responding. I know this may be a lot, and I promise you I am just trying to help make this thing we are trying to establish and build just a little easier on both of us. Thank

45   Nathan (@868nathan), "Ladies, no one will care more about your well-being than a guy you haven't heard from in months responding to your new swimsuit posts," Twitter, August 6, 2019, 5:47 p.m.

you for coming to this segment of my TED Talk, up next we talk to the men in the back. Yes sir, you.

Finally, sir, I just need to talk to some of you.

### YOU SIR, IN THE BACK—CAN WE HELP YOU?

Truly, I want this section to be a teaching moment, a vulnerable moment of understanding on both sides for us. Ladies, let's be real, we could probably write a whole separate book on the things that make us inhale and exhale that exasperated sigh constantly about the random things that men do every day. (I know, you just thought about something that the young man you are involved with does. And did you make that sighing sound? See, I know what I'm talking about.)

For research purposes, I asked the women I know about some things that men do that frustrate them, or what patterns they have that just make us wonder about their species. I asked women with a wide range of relationship statuses: married, in a relationship, dating. So no, it's not all bitter single women. The top responses were. . .

1. Exist: This one came courtesy of two of my friends, and I must admit that the question why some of you exist is truly valid. Is your main goal just to make women's lives difficult? Do you enjoy seeing what happens to her face when you push her buttons, or do you just have a death wish and would like to cease existing?

2. Breathe: Some of the men in the world are taking up oxygen they don't deserve. You can @ me at my statement. Meet me outside, I don't care!

That was funny, I made myself laugh. Ok now, in all seriousness.

1. Why do men call you cute one moment, but if you turn them down, why do they want to call out your name?

Answer easy: Fragile ego. I am not sure if all of you got the memo, but it was definitely broadcasted. I am allowed to say no to your advances. The same way I can come up to you as a woman and you can say no. However, I would never disrespect you in such a manner by calling you a bitch or ugly just because of a "no."

I have walked down the street and had a guy come up to me and start the usual spiel of how I'm pretty and ask me why I'm out here alone. Answer: I'm trying to get home. I tried to politely turn him down, but he wouldn't quit. I had to say no again, and then he called me a bitch. How do I go from beautiful to bitch in 2.3 seconds flat? I have actually just started lying and saying that I have a boyfriend because apparently men take to the fact that you "belong" to someone else better than me as a woman "belonging" to herself and saying no.

2. Why can't men address their emotions?

This one I can blame on society and this forced upbringing that strong men can't be vulnerable, but that's bullshit, and I am here to tell you, communication and vulnerability are sexy. To me, it makes men approachable. Society has taught us a lie, that men have to carry everything, and that's not true. In a relationship, we are partners. I rock for you and you rock for me. I will be your superwoman when you need me, and needing someone is ok.

Instead of talking, they either just deflect or shut down. I understand that maybe talking doesn't help you, and that is ok. Just let me know at least.

3. Why are women labeled "emotional and complicated" when men are so much more emotional than us.

I am speaking on this from personal experience. When Jonathan and I were together, whenever I brought up an issue,

I was either overreacting or doing the most. The minute I did something wrong, he didn't want to speak to me for days.

My friend Ariana started talking to this guy, very low key. They met on a dating app and were trying to set up a time for their second date. Much like myself, Ariana has a crazy work schedule, which she expressed to him. He just didn't believe that she was busy. I know that we sometimes lie to get out of things, but that isn't Ariana's style. She will quickly tell you if she doesn't want to see you.

She told him that she was only available Saturday mornings, and then he just went off like a firework. He started questioning whether she was too busy to afford him any time (as though this isn't what she is trying to do now) or whether he was just too far back in the queue.

Wait! There's more.

He then tried to backpedal his feelings about the scheduling by saying "it's cool" because he was trying to focus on his ambitions right now but would still value her company once in a blue moon. However, if she could be straight with him. If she already has someone, logistics with too many parts can be a drag.

I didn't know whether to laugh or scream. Sir, she is just BUSY!

Guys, most times we are just busy, we too have bills. There was such a better way to go about this. Guys, y'all just don't know how to express your emotions, and this drives us crazy, and then we look like the emotional ones. I promise you, it's not always us.

If I didn't want to give you the chance, I would have just ignored your text or told you that. Simple. No one has the energy to schedule things and then flake, at least I don't.

4. The unsolicited messages and imagery

Have you ever been excited by an unsolicited dick pick? I mean, honestly, why do men believe that women want any part in this? If I wanted to see that, or if any woman for that matter wanted to, she would have just asked.

Not only is it creepy, but it is also quite degrading. That's that. Just don't do it!

5. Men are always asking women to smile.

I am entitled to have my resting bitch face if I want to. Maybe I am having a bad day, you don't know. I have a follow-up question. Why do none of you smile in your photos? Most of you have this "yea you see me," half smirk on your face in every photo. Sir, can you please relax and be genuinely happy? It's ok to show range, you know?

6. Honestly, why are y'all so annoying?

I just want to know, is it genetics, is it society, is it television? You know how back in the day, they used to blame music and video games for making kids act up, which, as a kid of the '90s, makes no sense to me. I grew up on Looney Tunes. Wile E. Coyote has been trying to kill and eat the Road Runner for years. You don't see me throwing dynamite around to get at someone.

Part of me truly does think it's unintentional because the Pisces in me wants to give you the benefit of the doubt. The frustrated woman in me, however, thinks you get some weird enjoyment out of it, and that I can't stand for.

I know I asked some thought-provoking questions. Now would be a great time to start thinking about those answers. We need some—and desperately. Feel free to collaborate and gather in small groups. Please, take your time; we want the answer to truly be a problem solver. I want us to bridge these gaps and thrive together as well as possible. Clearly audacity is free ninety-nine percent this year and has certainly been on sale for years. I think it's time to clear the air. All answers can be submitted to my IG, @nikki_akinyi. I look forward to hearing your input and dispersing it to the group. Thanks for coming to my TED Talk.

# THE GAME DOESN'T
# BENEFIT ANYONE

---

"When it comes to love, everyone agrees that 'playing games' is bad. Yet we all play them."[46]

Being part of this game of dating has taught me so much. If I truly wanted to play the game of dating the way it should be played, I could probably do a decent job, but as I have learned, this system of dating that we have going on doesn't benefit anyone.

Truthfully, in a way we are all victims, but on the flip side we are also perpetrators. Some of us are takers and some of us are givers. Givers tend to always find themselves hurt because they allowed someone to take too much. Who's at fault? The giver who "allowed" this to happen or the taker who had no boundaries? In this vicious cycle of giving and taking, a giver can become a taker based on the nonsense another taker has put them through. We are essentially living in a cycle of emotional abuse.

---

46  Dan Savage, "The Dating Game," *Forbes*, December 14, 2006.

I have had the privilege of talking in a purely conversational way with a guy in his forties about his dating life. He told me he didn't date women his age because they were too jaded. I asked him why he thought they are jaded. He explained that it probably had to do to with their past, but he didn't want to be blamed for what some other guy did.

Which, to his credit, I agreed with. We should not carry emotional baggage from one relationship to another. You can be cautious without it being something catastrophic. Out of curiosity, I did inquire about what he was like back in his twenties and early thirties, which is when I am sure the jadedness started being ingrained in these women. He admitted to being a player. I just stared at him with my usual incredulous look.

Yet, you wonder why she is jaded. It's a fault of your own doing. When men like you were younger, you played them, took advantage of them—it's a monster of your own making. Yet here we are continuing the cycle.

We don't have to wait until we are in our forties to see this. It is something I witness and recognize in myself now. Given my own less-than-stellar experiences in the last few years, I have found myself shocked when guys respond to messages and actually have a vested interest. My cousin went on a date with a guy, she talked about how kind he was and how he was such a gentleman, holding her door, really inquiring about her life, checking in on her just to make sure she's ok. When she speaks about him, you can hear the awe in her voice. At first, I was excited, but then I realized why am I excited about something that should be the bare minimum.

Why do we play everything so close to the chest, what are we hiding, what are we so afraid to lose? Why are we so afraid to feel? Like I said before, we were not created to be alone, so why are we constructing a dynamic that only works best for us?

None of us are perfect, we all have things we can learn and change about ourselves. Life isn't about perfection, it's about progression. How can we become a little better every day? Even recognizing a fault is a progression. There is no such thing as a perfect relationship; we are two works in progress coming together to progress further on in life.

There are always going to be the external factors: your family, society, your friends. This journey of dating starts with you, then you move on to figuring out the type of person you want to be with, finally returning to you by self-analyzing whether as that person would you want to be with you. I do not mean this in a superficial way. I mean this in a "it's time to expose ourselves" type of way. If you are rude to others, how do you expect to attract someone who is kind? Relationships are work that include working on ourselves.

Dating is scary and uncertain. It is easy to either want to shy away from it or do all you can to protect yourself. However, no one said love or the process of getting there had any guarantees. We just hoped that we could all at least be decent to one another through this journey. I think in the grand scheme of things, finding that R&B type of love is worth it. Even if I am way too much of an optimist for still believing in that, I do not care. I have learned to stay in my lane.

At the end of the day, I just want us all to love freely and openly without worrying about keeping up pretenses. Without thinking that one person is better than the other and to actually care for one another. The game can be changed, I'm not saying it's always going to be a win-win. Things will happen. We are humans dealing with other humans. I just want that the next time you think of your relationship status regardless of what it is, you know that you are not alone you have me and all those touched by this book rooting for you. It was great meeting you, hopefully we can have brunch again soon! Until next time!

# ACKNOWLEDGEMENTS

---

First, I would like to thank my mom and dad for constantly encouraging me to keep going and checking up on me! My mom has seen the potential in me since I was in elementary school. I am just thankful my parents never thought I was crazy.

Thank you to all my girls who allowed me to share pieces of their stories and journeys. Thank you to the men in my life for their vulnerability in allowing our shared stories to be front page as well.

Thank you to Toddchelle, Alexa, and Dani for reading through my work and giving me advice along the way. Shout out to Alexa because honestly without her, I do not think I would have ever actually taken the plunge to do this. Thank you for the Saturday morning boy talks at work and being a sound board when Damien was losing his mind.

Thank you to New Degree Press, especially Eric Koester, Kyra Davis, Elissa Graeser, and Erika Arroyo for making the endless notes on my iPhone into something I didn't think was possible.

Finally, thank you to all of you who picked up this book! I hope it brings you as much joy reading it as I had writing it.

# APPENDIX

---

**PART ONE: WELCOME TO DATING**

**The Setup**

Winch, Guy. "Loneliness Poses Greater Public Health Threat Than Obesity." *The Squeaky Wheel* (blog), *Psychology Today*, August 23, 2017. https://www.psychologytoday.com/us/blog/the-squeaky-wheel/201708/loneliness-poses-greater-public-health-threat-obesity.

**Who You Got?**

Angelou, Maya (@DrMayaAngelou). "I've Learned That People Will Forget What You Said, People Will Forget What You Did, but People Will Never Forget How You Made Them Feel." Twitter, September 2, 2018, 2:59 p.m. https://twitter.com/drmayaangelou/status/1036327789488734208?lang=en.

**Standards**

Blackwood, Emily. "Strong Women Don't Have 'Attitudes' - We Have STANDARDS." *Mind Journal*, October 19, 2020. https://themindsjournal.com/strong-women-standards/. Originally appeared on Yourtango.com.

Jaxn, Derrick. "My Thoughts on Guys Who Say 'I Need Me an Ayesha Curry.'" *Derrick Jaxn* (blog). June 16, 2017. https://derrickjaxn.com/blogs/tips/my-thoughts-on-guys-who-say-i-need-me-an-ayesha-curry-derrick-jaxn-derrick-jaxn.

Lee, Leah. "Why Setting Standards in a Relationship Is Something Mandatory," *herway*, July 6, 2020. https://herway.net/relationship/setting-standards-relationship-something-mandatory/.

*Merriam-Webster.com Dictionary.* s.v. "standard," Accessed February 10, 2021, https://www.merriam-webster.com/dictionary/standard.

*Think Like a Man DVD. Directed by Tim Story. New York, NY: Screen Gems, 2012.*

Todd, Michael (@iammiketodd). "Delayed Doesn't Mean Denied." Twitter, May 12, 2020, 3:18 p.m. https://twitter.com/iammiketodd/status/1260288183927005187?lang=en.

*Transformation Church.* "Rip Up Your List // (Part 1)." May 3, 2020. Video, 1:15:05. https://www.youtube.com/watch?v=88TTZg-Prtko.

**PART TWO: WHAT IS DATING?**
**What Does Dating Even Mean?**
Oxford Languages. "dating." Google Search. Google, 2021. https://www.google.com/search?q=%E2%80%9CDefine+Dating%2C&rlz=1C5CHFA_enUS921US921&sxsrf=ALeKk01-M_auANTvNIJhzEHdjS1Rohbdjw%3A1617281972155&ei=tMNlYLjrCISm1QG-3YQI&oq=%E2%80%9CDefine+Dating%2C&gs_

lcp=Cgdnd3Mtd2l6EAMyAggAMgIIADICCAAyAggAMgI-
IADICCAAyAggAMgIIADICCAAyAggAUOYcWOYcYPg-
faAFwAHgAgAGNAYgB8gGSAQMwLjKYAQCgAQGqAQd-
nd3Mtd2l6wAEB&sclient=gws-wiz&ved=0ahUKEwi4lc7rjN-
3vAhUEUzUKHb4uAQEQ4dUDCA0&uact=5.

Penthousepapi (@primehob). "Talking Stage 2 Years relationship
5 Years Engagement 3 Years Plan the Wedding 1.5 Years Get
Married." Twitter, June 13, 2020. https://twitter.com/primehob/
status/1271658515506122752?lang=en.

*Urban Dictionary.* "Dating." Accessed June 23, 2009. https://www.
urbandictionary.com/define.php?term=Dating.

**So, Do You Have A Boyfriend? The Family Edition**

Perrin, Amanda Brooke (@brookeperrin). "Real Convo: MOM: Are
You Dating Anyone? ME: No.MOM: (LONG ASS PAUSE) ...
Well, Are Your Friends Dating Anyone?." Twitter, September
20, 2017, 7:18 p.m. https://twitter.com/brookeperrin?lang=en.

Pugachevsky, Julia. "22 Jokes You'll Get If Your Family Constantly
Asks About Your Love Life." *Cosmopolitan*, December 26, 2017.
https://www.cosmopolitan.com/sex-love/a13819433/jokes-fam-
ily-asks-about-love-life/.

**This Generation Isn't For Me**

Gilmour, Paisley. "13 Ridiculously Cute Stories of How Couples
Met to Restore Your Faith in Love." *Cosmopolitan*, October
23, 2017. https://www.cosmopolitan.com/uk/love-sex/relation-
ships/a13068525/cute-relationship-stories/.

Sin, r.h (@rhsin). "she's evolving don't distract her." Instagram photo, July 9, 2019. https://www.instagram.com/r.h.sin/?hl=en.

**I Have Been Single So Long, I Feel Like I Am On Year-End Clearance**
"If You Find Yourself Constantly Trying to Prove Your Worth to Someone, You Have Already Forgotten Your Value." *Tiny Buddha*, last modified June 9, 2015. https://tinybuddha.com/wisdom-quotes/if-you-find-yourself-constantly-trying-to-prove-your-worth-to-someone-you-have-already-forgotten-your-value/.

Nova, Kaya (@thekayanova). "I noticed when I tell people about dating issues they immediately say" but you're so amazing! Your person is coming or you're so beautiful, its gonna happen! "And I just have to ask since when have women being amazing or beautiful guaranteed us a safe, fulfilled dating life?" Twitter, June 29, 2020, 3:57 p.m. https://twitter.com/thekayanova/status/1277692743108702208

**PART THREE: HOW DATING WORKS IF YOU ARE GOING TO DO IT?**
**Looking for Love**
Fequiere, Pedro. "21 Times Animals Proved To Be The Best Things On The Internet." *Buzzfeed*, July 13, 2018. https://www.buzzfeed.com/pedrofequiere/21-tweets-with-animals-that-will-blow-your-mind-or-crack?utm_source=dynamic&utm_campaign=bffb-buzzfeed&ref=bffbbuzzfeed&fbclid=IwAR3IMkjUpWG251nfuzN-MAw1DqqosParfontW2YThT3OiSZG_ooUPeuKBscE

sWooZie (@sWooZie). "I Ain't Nobodys Plan B. Either You Choose Me or You Lose Me." Twitter, September 11, 2012, 5:58 p.m. https://twitter.com/swoozie/status/245642492400242689?lang=en.

## The Apps

LaScala, Marisa. "If You're Sick of Being Single, It's Time to Download a New Dating App." *Good Housekeeping,* July 17, 2020. https://www.goodhousekeeping.com/life/relationships/g30730909/best-dating-apps2020/.

## Ghosting

Murray, Megan. "Online dating: soft ghosting is the exasperating trend that just won't quit." *Stylist,* December 29, 2020. https://www.stylist.co.uk/life/online-dating-app-trend-for-millennials-soft-ghosting/301880.

*Urban Dictionary.* "Ghosting."

Accessed August 19, 2020. https://www.urbandictionary.com/define.php?term=Ghosting.

## Can Men and Women Just Be Friends?

Borresen, Kelsey. "In Preschool, He Told His Class He Would Marry Her. And Then He Did." *HuffPost,* June 28, 2017. https://www.huffpost.com/entry/guy-marries-his-preschool-crush_n_5952bb3ee4b02734df2e1cf4.

Celine, Mollie. "I Know He's Not My Boyfriend - but He's Still Mine. Tagalog Love Quotes, Hes Mine Quotes, Back off Quotes." Pinterest, January 23, 2021. https://www.pinterest.com/pin/472174342153377374/.

## Shoulda, Woulda, Coulda

Katz, Evan Marc. "Should Women Ask Men Out on First Dates?" *Dating Coach - Evan Marc Katz | Understand Men. Find*

*Love*, January 18, 2021. https://www.evanmarckatz.com/blog/ dating-tips-advice/should-women-ask-men-out-on-first-dates.

Vartan, Starre. "Why More Women Should Ask Men Out on Dates." *Treehugger*, Accessed October 6, 2020. https://www. treehugger.com/starre-vartan-4845361.

Wong, Brittany. "Women On Twitter Are Sharing What Happens When They Ask Crushes Out On A Date." *HuffPost*, October 27, 2017. https://www.huffpost.com/entry/women-are-tweeting-what-happens-when-they-ask-their-crushes-outn59f360d3e4b-03cd20b8150c3.

### It Just Happened

Fans, Sza (@itssza). "My last relationship taught me A LOT. It taught me not to ignore signs & my gut feeling. I learned how to love myself & not to put anyone above my happiness & my dreams. Now I know my worth, know what I want, & I won't settle for less again. No regrets, I needed to learn those lessons." Twitter, February 2, 2018, 2:36 p.m. https://twitter.com/itssza/status/959510789777494018.

Quint, Bella (@bellaquintt). ""She said…He was never mine but losing him broke my heart" I felt that." Twitter, December 1, 2020, 3:06 a.m. https://twitter.com/bellaquintt/status/1333683768175915010.

### PART FOUR: NOW WHAT?

### Intimacy versus Sex

*Merriam-Webster.com Dictionary*. s.v. "intimacy," Accessed January 28, 2021. https://www.merriam-webster.com/dictionary/intimacy.

**Me versus My Ovaries**

"13 Legitimate Reasons Why Women Are Freezing Their Eggs." *Elanza Wellness,* Last updated May 12, 2020. https://www.elanzawellness.com/post/14-reasons-why-women-are-freezing-their-eggs.

Byer, Nicole and Whitney Cummings. "Emojis are a Red Flag." December 13, 2019. *In Why Won't You Date Me.* Produced by HeadGum. Podcast, MP3 Audio. https://podcasts.apple.com/ca/podcast/emojis-are-a-red-flag-w-whitney-cummings/id1314759544?i=1000459495443.

Byer, Nicole and Deray Davis. "Making a Polyamorous Relationship Work." July 26, 2019. In *Why Won't You Date Me.* Produced by HeadGum. Podcast, MP3 Audio, 3:54https://podcasts.apple.com/us/podcast/making-a-polyamorous-relationship-work-w-deray-davis/id1314759544?i=1000445358643.

**Dating as a Chocolate Girl**

Count Your Blessings Yt Girl (@LilHeffeBarbie). ""The fact that Black women are praying they find a Black man that protects them, the way Harry protects Meghan REALLY says a lot." Twitter, Accessed March 9, 2021, 12:03 p.m. https://twitter.com/lilheffabarbie?lang=en.

**If Winnie the Pooh Can Wear a Crop Top, I Can Too!**

Byer, Nicole. December 2017. In *Why Won't You Date Me.* Produced by HeadGum (2017-2021) and Team Coco (2021-Present), podcast. https://podcasts.apple.com/us/podcast/why-wont-you-date-me-with-nicole-byer/id1314759544.

Byer, Nicole and Gay, Roxane. "Fatphobia." August 7, 2020. In *Why Won't You Date Me.* Produced by HeadGum. Podcast,

MP3 Audio. https://podcasts.apple.com/us/podcast/fatpho-bia-w-roxane-gay/id1314759544?i=1000487392034.

Hazlehurst, Beatrice. "Rihanna: You Want to Have a Butt, Then You Have a Gut.'" *Paper,* June 15, 2020. https://www.papermag.com/rihanna-body-shamers-2591849841.html

Holly Bross. "100 Quotes Ideas: Quotes, Inspirational Quotes, Me Quotes." Pinterest, December 4, 2018. https://www.pinterest.com/.

Nunes, Mary. "It's True: The Average Size of the American Woman Is No Longer 14." *Byrdie,* December 22, 2020. https://www.byrdie.com/average-body-weight.

**QTNA: Questions That Need Answers**
Jalili, Candice. "'If You Don't Love Me At My" Memes Are Taking Over Twitter & I'm Pee-Laughing." *Elite Daily,* April 4, 2018. https://www.elitedaily.com/p/if-you-dont-love-me-at-my-memes-are-taking-over-twitter-im-pee-laughing-8690337.

Nathan (@868nathan). "Ladies, no one will care more about your well being than a guy you haven't heard from in months responding to your new swimsuit posts." Twitter, August 6, 2019, 5:46 p.m. https://twitter.com/868nathan/status/1158902556506169349.

**The Game Doesn't Benefit Anyone**
Savage, Dan. "The Dating Game." *Forbes,* December 14, 2006. https://www.forbes.com/2006/12/10/games-dating-relationships-tech-cx_ds_games06_1212savage.html?sh=3a4603f45daf.

9 781636 768397